ADOPTION'S HIDDEN HISTORY:

FROM NATIVE AMERICAN TRIBES

TO LOCKED LIVES

(VOLUME ONE)

By

Mary S. Payne

Adoption's Hidden History:

From Native American Tribes to Locked Lives

Volume One

© 2013 Mary S. Payne

Manufactured in the United States of America.

ISBN: 1482651262

ISBN-13:9781482651263

Cover: by Paul Beeley

http://www.create-imaginations.com

FOR MORE INFORMATION AND UPDATES, SEE:

http://www.adoptionshiddenhistory.com

DEDICATION

For Sylvia and Darlene

in memory of Steven,

their birth son and brother

For adult adoptees SuzAnne and Pat

and all other individuals

impacted by adoption

May you find peace and your heart's desire.

ACKNOWLEDGEMENTS

Gratitude is owed to more librarians than I can name. Each one worked tirelessly to help pull together the materials used in this work. I will be forever grateful. A special thank you goes to the interlibrary loan personnel of the Pioneer Library System of Cleveland County, Oklahoma.

Friday Writers of Norman, Oklahoma, Kathleen Park and others helped to edit the manuscript, although any errors belong solely with the author.

I wish to thank a number of individuals and institutions who graciously allowed me to reprint pictures and quotations. They are the Department of Rare Books and Special Collections-University of Rochester Library, Gelman Library's Special Collections-George Washington University, Archdiocese of Oklahoma City, the Oklahoma Publishing Company, Scripps-Howard Newspapers, the Peabody Museum of Archaeology and Ethnology-Harvard, Library of Congress, Kansas State Historical Society, Oklahoma Historical Society, Opal Bennington Clark, the Children's Home and Aid Society of Illinois, the Mahn Center for Archives and

Special Collections-Ohio University Library, Edmond Historical Society and Museum, and the Oklahoma State Archives. These permissions do not constitute endorsement of any viewpoint proposed by the author in this manuscript. Other quoted material appears here under the fair use doctrine.

Thanks to my family for their unwavering support over the last 20 years as this project materialized. Mike Payne's computer expertise has been invaluable.

CONTENTS

PREFACE

Adoptions are finalized daily across America. This cultural phenomenon—making a child your own who is not your own—developed over centuries. Like the root system of tall trees, adoption history lies buried in decades of human events, hiding its foundation from the world.

I learned about adoption when I was five years old. Little did I know that the next few moments would place me on a path searching for self and questioning my very existence. Every child has to have a birth certificate to enroll in kindergarten.

I was so excited about going to school. There would be lots of kids to play with. My parents were older, and I was an only child—so I didn't have any playmates. It would be exciting to talk to other kids. On the day before I was to enroll, I was in the bedroom with my mother. She was sewing school clothes for me. It was warm and the windows were open. The sweet smell of honeysuckle wafted through the screen. The whir-r-r of the sewing machine stopped. She said she had something very important to talk to me about. I couldn't imagine what that might be.

She pointed to a toddler-sized wicker rocker. "Sit right there, Mary."

I sat down in the rocker and leaned back, looking up at her. I felt so small on that tiny chair with my head tilted back to see her face. She picked up a piece of paper. "I need to tell you something. We're not your real parents. You were born to a different mother and father. They couldn't keep you, so we got you when you were eighteen months old."

My gut felt like it had been punched. My shoulders slumped, nearly dumping me out of the chair. "What did you say? What happened? What was wrong with me?"

Looking back, I think I went into shock. She pointed to the paper, which I later learned was my amended birth certificate. It's a piece of paper that says people who are not related to you are your legal parents. I couldn't read, but she read it to me. She said my original birth certificate was sealed by state law and I would never have it. Never?

When I was older, I asked my dad about the amended birth certificate. He said, "Your life began when we adopted you!" But it didn't answer any of my questions. The amended birth certificate verifies that I was adopted. It does not verify I was born. There is no information about my actual birth. I am grateful to my adoptive parents, but it does not take away the pain of not knowing the history of who I am. I hid away the hurt...and pondered those things in my heart.

Years later, during an adult adoptee support group meeting, a young woman, who had been adopted through an Oklahoma maternity home, came to share. We connected right away. She introduced me to a birth mother, who had lived at the Mae

Marshall Private Home for Unfortunate Girls in 1953 and was forced to relinquish her son Steven. We got together to look for clues into the operation of the unwed mothers' home.

I began to wonder how adoption could have developed with so little coherent planning. What could have sparked the idea of sealing original birth certificates? It didn't seem fair. Were adult adoptees second-class citizens? Birth certificates belong to the subject of the record—how could they presume the initial record of my birth was an unimportant thing? I wanted to know the exact time, date and place of birth, rather than the false specifics others wanted me to believe about myself.

It's the twenty-first century. It's time to know how this policy came to be!

By reading thousands of newspaper microfilm pages and hundreds of public records, I pieced together the story--how adoption moved from Native American Indian tribes to state capitols, to the courts and to maternity homes.

Come join me in a walk through time to explore adoption's past and learn the way it developed in our American society.

PART A: FROM CONCEPT TO LEGALIZATION

CHAPTER 1

EARLY AMERICAN INDIANS

The adoption procedure for each adoptee in the United States is based on thousands of public and private historical events, changes of attitude and court processes occurring over the last 300 years. Some were major events receiving extensive publicity, but most were small decisions, often unnoticed by the general public.

Its history began as Native American Indians practiced adoption on American soil long before Europeans colonized New England. The tribes accepted adoption as a normal part of their heritage and culture.

Two founders of the Iroquois Confederacy, Deganawida and Hiawatha, are said to have been adopted as adults into the Mohawk Tribe in the northeastern United States. Sketches of their lives have passed through generations of Indian storytellers.

A young girl and her mother were part of the Wendats, a small division of the Huron Tribe. They lived by themselves, because all other family members had died.

When the girl's mid-section began to increase, the mother chided her for the pregnancy.

"I don't know how it happened," she told her mother.

Anger took over the mother's personality. She could not put the negative emotion aside. When Deganawida was born, "Grandma" tried three times to kill him.

The young mother devoted her life to protecting her son. He grew up to be a sensitive, caring young man.

Deganawida viewed the Indian way of violence with disdain. He believed his life's mission was to unite the Indian tribes into a council that would settle disputes by negotiation, rather than by war. He built a canoe and journeyed south into the land of the Mohawk Tribe, where he came upon Hiawatha, a leader of the Onondaga people.

Chief Hiawatha's journey into Mohawk territory was personal. He sought solace.

Hiawatha told himself that he must go where he would not be reminded of his three daughters who died.

His grief was all-consuming and the Mohawk people wanted to help him feel better. Members of the tribe adopted Hiawatha and Deganawida, so the men would feel a sense of belonging, while they camped near their villages.

The two men forged a partnership for the purpose of blending five of the northeastern tribes into one unit. The tribes were the Iroquois, Mohawk, Seneca, Onondaga, and Cayuga. (1) They laid the framework for the organization of the league and persuaded the tribal chiefs of each tribe to join.

The Constitution of the Iroquois Confederacy, or Five Nations, authorized adoptions. Any member or family from any of the five Indian tribes could submit a proposal to be adopted, furnishing a string of shells as a record and a pledge to the clan into which they wished to be adopted. The elders would then vote on the proposal. Any member who wished to adopt an individual, family, or families was required to offer adoption to the prospective adoptee.

When the offer was accepted, the prospective adoptive parents would ask the elders to confirm the adoption. Once it was approved, a new name, called "A name hung about the neck," was chosen. Foreshadowing today's sealed record policy, the Indians believed the original names should never again be used, because doing so would cause a rift between the two families or tribes.

When a visitor arrived in an Indian camp, he was often adopted into the tribe during a ritual called the Ceremony of the Calumet, or Peace Pipe. This was to show the visitor how much his hosts honored him. Gifts were exchanged to validate their statements of feeling for each other.

The elders of the Iroquois Confederacy were also allowed to declare war on other tribes and peoples to gain territory or to take captives who could later be adopted into the tribes to replace lost relatives. (2)

In 1648, the Iroquois voted to take over the territory of the Huron Tribe. As the war dragged on, there was no place for the Huron refugees to hide. The Onondaga Tribe adopted approximately 1,000 Huron individuals into their tribe. In some cases, an entire family or village was "adopted." Others traveled west, changing the name of their tribe from Huron to Wyandotte. (3) By 1660, in spite of their numbers being augmented by captives and adopted individuals, manpower in the Confederacy was declining. When a person died through warfare or illness, there was pressure to go to war to replace him with another individual to perform his duties in the family and for the tribe. (4)

One of the first recorded Indian raids where white captives were taken by Indians and later adopted occurred in 1690. French soldiers offered the Indians a bounty for each Puritan they could take captive at Salmon Falls. A number of warriors joined the soldiers for the three-month journey south, across the snow-covered mountains and frozen streams of northern New Hampshire, to the settlement of Salmon Falls.

After the massacre, many captives died on the return trip, some from the arduous trek itself, and others from the quick temper of the Indians.

Once the Indians and captives arrived back at the village, some of the harsh treatment ended, although the prospect of torture still hung heavily over the prisoners' heads. The captives were treated as slaves and given the least desirable jobs in the village. Far from their own families, their chance of being rescued was between slim and none. Most captives wished to be adopted, if only to rise from the position of slave.

Richard Slotkin described Indian adoption of that time period in his book, *Regeneration through Violence: Mythology of the American Frontier, 1600-1860*:

At least since the coming of the white man, north-eastern Indian tribes had traditionally augmented their numbers by adopting captive children and marrying captive women...Orphaned children, whose parents had been killed by the Indians, were adopted into the tribe, by bereft Indian parents and raised with all the openness of affection and depth of concern they would have given to a child of their own blood or a similarly adopted child of a deceased relation. (5)

The Indian adoption ceremony is spiritually linked to the mourning process, according to Robert L. Hall's *An Archaeology of the Soul: North American Indian Belief and Ritual*. The adoptee "symbolically reincarnates as a deceased tribesman…to take his place in the spiritual sense." (6)

Many Indian tribes believed the soul of their deceased relative could not rest until someone had been adopted who would take his place, and perhaps, his name.

When French explorer Robert LaSalle visited the Miami Indians in 1681, he was given gifts of cloth and beaver skins. He extolled the virtues of their Chief Ouabicolcata, who had died in a battle with the Iroquois. According to the Indian custom, he spoke to them as their reincarnated chief:

> I have his mind and soul in my own body. I am going to revive his name and be another Ouabicolcata…his family shall want for nothing, since his soul is entered into the body of a Frenchman. (7)

Although this account was written by LaSalle, Hall believes it is consistent with the Indian adoption ceremony.

Lewis Henry Morgan, a lawyer and the first American archaeologist, laboriously studied the Iroquois culture. His interest was sparked by the Seneca Indians, who lived in the general vicinity of Aurora, New York, his boyhood home. Morgan believed that by studying all primitive cultures, he would find similarities in their social organizations, which could mean everyone was descended from the same ancestors.

While browsing in a bookstore, Morgan met Ely Parker, a young Seneca Indian who was willing to answer questions about his tribe. He introduced Morgan to various leaders who could expand his knowledge about the formation of the tribe. (8)

Spending hours, days and weeks away from his law practice, Morgan diligently structured the Indian kinship system and wrote extensively on all aspects of Indian life.

Morgan's first book, *The League of the Ho-de-no-sau-nee, or Iroquois*, published in Rochester in 1851, described the personal characteristics of the Iroquois Indians, as well as their social organization. Morgan was impressed with the spirit of hospitality within the Indian culture. He states, "Their houses were not only open to each other, at all hours of the day and of the night, but also to the wayfarer and the stranger." (9)

In addition, the Indians are a truthful people, Morgan wrote. "On all occasions, and at whatever peril, the Iroquois spoke the truth without fear and without hesitation." (10)

Morgan described the process of adopting captives who were taken in war. The two alternatives for the captive were adoption or death. Male captives were forced to run through the gauntlet, while being whipped at every hand. If a captive fell during this part of the ordeal, he was automatically deemed unworthy and sentenced to death. The captives who survived the gauntlet were assigned new names and adopted publicly. (11)

Morgan's biographer, Carl Reser, described his research into the Iroquois' family customs. Each tribe was divided into eight clans: Wolf, Bear, Beaver, Turtle, Deer, Snipe, Heron and Hawk. Members of the same clan could not marry, and the children were always members of the mother's clan. A son inherited nothing from his father, not even his tomahawk. Another distinct custom was how the Indians described their kin:

> They merged collateral relatives...an Iroquois child used the same term when referring to its mother's sisters as it did when referring to its mother. All were equally "mothers," a grandmother and her sisters equally "grandmothers." Conversely, the children of two or more sisters were the "sons" and "daughters" of all, without distinction, and called each other "brothers" and "sisters." The same held true in the male line. (12)

Reser also reports Morgan and two friends, Charles Porter and Thomas Darling, asked to be adopted into the Seneca Tribe. There was some conflict among the chiefs over the request, but they were reminded how Morgan had lobbied for the tribe in Washington. The chiefs agreed to adopt the three men after the prospective adoptees offered to pay the cost of the food for the feast, which followed the ceremony. (13)

Morgan described his 1847 adoption ceremony in a subsequent book, *Ancient Societies*. (14)

The earliest known written adoption ritual is titled "Initiation Ceremony." It is located among Morgan's papers at the University of Rochester.

The Seneca Prophet begins the ceremony with a speech:

Our scouts have again been on the war-path and have brought in this young captive who has wandered so long among the pale-faces, as to have lost nearly every trace of his parentage and descent from our ancient Nation; but the unceasing vigilance of our Indian band has excelled us to penetrate the obscurity which hung over his footsteps and to discover within him those elements of character, which distinguish him as one worthy of joining us upon this most western war-path of the Confederacy and as one well qualified to aid us in guarding the western door of the House of the Iroquois. It now comes my duty as the Prophet of the…Ho-de-no-sau-nee to present him to you, most renowned Sachem, for regeneration and adoption as a brother and as a Seneca. (15)

Then, the Sachem (a chief of the tribe) spoke:

Young warriors. Possess your mind in peace. We have opened our ears and listened to the voice of the Prophet in your behalf. [sic] We have considered your claims to a seat beside the Council Fire of the Senecas and have concluded to receive you as a warrior into the Order of the Iroquois. But first that you may comprehend the duties you are about to assume; and understand the nature of the Confederation into which you are this night to be inducted. Know then, young warrior, that many years before the pale-face set his foot upon this western world, (the Indians) formed a great perpetual confederacy and named it the Indian Nation of the Iroquois. Their broad territories extended nearly from the rising to the setting sun and all the Indian races on this great continent acknowledged their supremacy. But after many generations of prosperity, the pale-face came among them and raised his exterminating hand. The Great Spirit could not avert their destiny and the Iroquois visually proceeded away before the rising influence of the new race, and many moves have now lapsed over since the ancient confederacy of the Iroquois was broken up. Young warrior, continue to listen. A new day at last has dawned and the Confederacy of the Iroquois has been renewed. It is now moving onward, strengthening its union, increasing its warriors, and enlarging its boundaries. Even this night the Council Fire of the Oneida burns brightly upon the hills of the Oneida toward the rising sun. The hunting grounds of the Onondagas are again occupied by their Sachem and the chiefs. While the Cayugas upon the eastern shores of this bright and beautiful lake are even now assembled in their Council Chambers...Also at the banks of the rivers of the Senecas as with ourselves are now in the Council and to a brief period, the warriors of the Order of the Iroquois will come upon a hill and rally the ancient confederacy.

Young warriors, mark the words of the Prophet, who will now administer the oath of secrecy and fidelity. (16)

The Prophet continued the ceremony:

Young warrior. You are about to take upon you the vows of the Seneca. It is a serious and sober matter. It is a serious and solemn undertaking. We are not engaged in a trifle or transitory object, but one of deep and absorbing interest and we do expect from you here-after a vigorous and spirited assistance not only at our festivals, but also in our labors, which are many fold and unending. Do you promise to render it? ['I do.']

Do you also pledge yourself in the presence of the Great Spirit whose eye beholdeth us on this occasion, never to divulge the secrets of our Order, which may now or hereafter be entrusted to your keeping, to sustain them in the spirit of rectitude and of honor, you, with the Red Man's faith? ['I do']

Then, as you hold this pledge, you will be respected and devoted and receive all our confidence, but on the other hand, if in an idle hour…you should dare to lift the veil of secrecy from our order and expose it to the pale-face, a retribution, the very thought of which would make you shudder even in the grave, will follow quick with your every footstep. The Senecas never abandon a friend, neither do they ever forgive or forget an enemy or betrayer. But, young warrior, we anticipate no evil from you, we have sanctionized your claims to our fellowship and we are satisfied that our confidence will be safely secured. We give you a cordial welcome to our Council Fire and at all times hereafter we should greet you upon our hunting grounds as brother and Seneca.

Sachem, chiefs, and warriors of the Turtle Tribe of the Seneca: Do you receive this man as an adopted warrior? [War-whoops] (17)

Morgan described the conclusion of the ceremony, "The bandage is removed. The warrior, stand(s) in perfect silence and rest(s) in their love. After a minute, the Prophet leads the novice toward the Sachem before whom he kneels." (18)

The Sachem reaches out his hand to the initiate:

This is the grip by which thou shalt know a brother. Mark it well. Thou shalt hereafter be known on the war-path by the name of _____. Let thy conduct—enterprise, fidelity and zeal—render this apellation [sic] renowned away from the Seneca warriors of the Gennessee. (19)

The Sachem, Prophet, and novitiate stand together in the center. The head warrior leads the band around them in a march, singing the war-song. When the music stops, the Sachem introduces (each one with his) Indian name to the novitiate, who gives to him in turn the grip. Afterwards, there are congratulations, singing and dancing, refreshments and merriment. (20)

Morgan's work attracted the attention of John Wesley Powell, the director of the U. S. Geological Survey.

Powell was intensely interested in anything about Indians. A one-armed Civil War veteran, he distinguished himself as the leader of a rag-tag band of adventurers whose dangerous mission was to map the ferocious Colorado River by canoe. No one had ever run the rapids and lived to tell the tale. Powell actually made two trips down the Colorado River. His interpreter for the second expedition was Jacob Hamblin, a Mormon, who lived close to the Indians for a considerable period of time. He had a number of children. Some of them were his natural children, and some were adopted. Hamblin thought his life's mission was to cultivate peace between the Indians and white people. (21)

Powell believed that studying Indian culture and publishing the findings would reduce fear and misunderstanding between the two cultures. (22) Hamblin introduced Powell to many of the Indians who lived in the region where they were to embark on their journey. In 1870, they spent two months living with these Indians and learning their culture.

When Powell returned to Washington, his notes were the only source of scientific information about the Grand Canyon and the region surrounding it. He was named the first director of the U. S. Geological Survey. In addition to his duties with the Geological Survey, Powell was named head of the Bureau of Ethnology, a research arm of the Smithsonian Institution. He accumulated and published all kinds of data on the American Indians. While the actual staff of the bureau remained small, Powell fostered the careers of many researchers and published their findings.

Powell's most notable writer in the area of Indian adoptions was Alice Cunningham Fletcher. She has been called the first woman anthropologist. A white woman who never married, she informally adopted an Omaha Indian who worked as a clerk in the Treasury Department in 1891. Fletcher and Francis LaFlesche lived together as mother and son until her death in 1923. Their home at 214 First Street in Washington, D.C., became a meeting place for many anthropologists and Indians from near and far. LaFlesche introduced her to many members of his tribe, and she lived with his family in Nebraska for a period of time while she was gathering information. He served as her research assistant. Fletcher's biographer, Joan Mark, said LaFlesche decided at the last minute not to formalize the adoption, because he didn't want to lose his last name. (23)

Perhaps Fletcher believed LaFlesche filled a vacant place in her life, much as a captive of the Osages filled a vacant spot in the lives of Indian parents.

According to her research, when a captive was held for adoption, the captor invited a group of tribal chiefs to attend a special meeting. After food was served, the host gave a solemn speech. He declared that he wished to adopt his captive. The group sent for men who were familiar with the ritual and would take part in the ceremony.

When everyone was crowded into the lodge, the captive was brought in to sit at the place opposite to the door—the place of the stranger. A ritual was given which was used for a child born into the tribe. It was followed by stories, telling the history of the tribe and the four stages of a man's life. The captive was passed to the chief of peace on the north and then to the chief of war on the south side of the tent, symbolizing that he was to share in all aspects of their life.

The chief of war slashed the captive's nose with a sharp-pointed knife, causing blood to flow. Another chief wiped away the blood. A third chief cleaned the wound, while another gave the individual food.

A sacred peace pipe was filled and ceremoniously smoked by the captive.

Buffalo fat was spread over the captive's body. When two black stripes were painted across his face, the chief announced the captive's new name, Ni'wathe, which means "made to live." The adoption was complete.

Fletcher explained the ceremony this way:

The letting of blood symbolized that the captive lost the blood and kinship tribe into which he had been born. All traces of his former birth were removed by the washing away of the blood. He was then given food by those in the tribe who led the hunt…the new blood made by the Osage food was thus made Osage blood.

This symbolic act was confirmed and sanctified by the smoking of the pipe…The anointing of the body brought the captive entirely within the rites and avocations of the tribe. The black stripes (on the face) were in recognition of the Thunder as the god of war and the captive's future duties as a warrior of the tribe…this drama represents the death of the captive not only to the people of his birth, but to his past life, and his rebirth into the family of the Osage who saved him and "made" him "to live" by adopting him.

At the close of the ceremony, the chiefs who had taken part in the rites partook of the feast which the man who adopted the captive had provided for the occasion. Not long after, the name Ni'wathe was dropped and the adopted child without further ceremony was given a name belonging to the father's group. (24)

Fletcher's largest adoption project was transcribing an intertribal adoption ceremony, called the "Hako." The term is derived from two words, akow and rukkis. Akow is from the word mouth and rukkis means wood. The "h" symbolizes the breath. The whole ritual itself means a "breathing mouth of wood." (25) The Hako originated in a dream, given to the Indians' forefathers.

It was in a vision that our fathers were told how they could cause a man who was not their bodily offspring to become a Son, to be bound to them by a tie as strong as the natural tie between father and son. For this knowledge our fathers gave thanks and we give thanks, for by this ceremony, peace and plenty, strength, and all good things come to the people. (26)

Fletcher spent 15 years searching for a person who knew this ceremony. When she became acquainted with a man named Tahirussawichi, he was 70 years old. His whole life work had been devoted to the maintenance of the ceremonies of the Chaui band of the Pawnee Tribe. As a young man, Tahirussawichi had been instructed in the meaning and use of all of the ceremonies and their sacred objects. When the adoption ceremony was performed, it took five days. Fletcher and LaFlesche spent four years transcribing it.

The Hako is performed by people from two different tribes, or from two different clans within the same tribe. One group represents the fathers and the other group represents the sons. The fathers bring gifts and the sons provide a location for the ceremony.

One man is chosen to represent the father, and another man in the second unit is chosen to be the son. The selection of the individual who is to be the Son is taken very seriously. All the chiefs in the father's tribe are consulted. It must be someone who is respected within his own tribe, or clan. The Indians believed this ceremony brings long life and makes his family strong. This ritual forever binds the two immediate families of the father and son together.

The fathers gather gifts together for the son and they form a procession to find him. An ear of corn, which symbolizes "Mother Corn," is carried by the "father," who leads the way to the son. The corn represents fertility and the Indian's dependence on nature. During the procession, everyone sings, praising the wonderful features of the land. They also contemplate the bounty of Mother Corn and the all-power of Tirawa, their name for God.

When the "son" is found, he is painted and given new clothing and other gifts, because that is what a loving father would do. Two young men perform a ritual dance with the peace pipes. At its conclusion, the pipes are smoked to symbolize the merging of the two groups into an adoptive relationship and a symbolic blood tie.

Fletcher notes that many different tribes used this ceremony, but it does not appear to be a ceremony for actually adopting captives. (27)

Let's turn now to the life stories of captive individuals, who were adopted into Indian families.

CHAPTER 2

TALES OF INDIAN CAPTIVITIES

Numerous tales of adopted Indian captives have been published throughout American history. The public devoured these stories of adventure, mystery, and triumph-over-the-odds. They helped set the stage for the acceptance of the legal process of adoption.

Daniel Boone—adopted by Shawnee Indians

The first account of Daniel Boone's captivity and adoption into the Shawnee Tribe was published in John Filson's "The Discovery, Settlement and Present State of Kentucke" in 1784. (28) James Fennimore Cooper further developed the tale in *The Last of the Mohicans.*

Filson, for his part, was a schoolteacher turned land speculator, surveyor, and finally author. Boone was his Kentucky guide. Over the campfire, the white frontiersman and former captive shared the story of his Indian adventures with his audience of one, who transcribed the story.

Roughly, Boone was captured by Shawnees and marched to Fort Detroit, where the British were purchasing some of the prisoners. The Shawnees were so pleased with Boone that they refused to sell him. He was adopted into an Indian family. He had Indian parents, brothers, and sisters, who treated him as an equal. He was so esteemed that they trusted him enough to hunt game unattended.

When Boone realized the Indians were planning an assault on Kentucky, he ran away to warn white Boonesborough settlers of the impending attack. Boone led the pioneers through this ordeal, pushing back 400 Indians who laid siege to the camp.

Matthew Brayton—adopted by "Snake Indians"

Wyandot County, Ohio, was the scene of one family's tragedy, involving the loss of their son. (29) Searchers found no trace of seven-year-old Matthew Brayton. After an exhaustive manhunt, they called off the search, concluding the boy had been carried off into slavery by a renegade band of Canadian Indians.

Matthew had been rounding up some cattle with his brother William. When the younger boy grew tired, William allowed him to go to a neighbor's farmhouse to play. Matthew had only walked a short way when a band of Indians, who had a grudge against the white settlers in the area, snatched him off the wooded path.

These Indians sold Matthew to a party of Pottawatomies in Michigan. Later, he was traded to the Paw-Paws for five-and-a-half gallons of whiskey. Over a period of several years, he was sold to the Winnebagos, the Chippewas, and the Sioux.

While Matthew was traveling with a band of Sioux, they met a party of Snake Indians. The Indians celebrated their meeting with a great Dog Dance.

After the dance, the Snake Indians purchased Matthew for 11 gallons of whiskey. An Indian couple, whose son had been killed in battle, adopted him as their own son. Matthew journeyed on foot with his new tribe from Iowa to Missouri and then they pushed west through Utah to California. Although Matthew's adoptive parents loved him, he was required to do much of the drudgery work usually assigned to the women.

The Snake chief tattooed Matthew to brand him as an Indian. He gave him his daughter to wed. The couple had one son.

The chief sent Matthew with a group of braves to an agency to ask for food and supplies. Despite the tattoo, one of the traders recognized Matthew's white features. When the Indian agent talked to Matthew about his parentage, Matthew insisted he was Indian. The band left the agency without any more supplies, rather than risk losing Matthew.

The adopted Indian was mystified by this behavior. He wondered if there were other parents "somewhere out there."

Blackfoot Indians attacked the group as they headed home. After a fierce battle, Matthew's group retreated to a campsite beside a river to rest for a few days before hitting the trail again.

Traders in a nearby village also recognized Matthew's white features. Although Matthew was seven years old when he was taken, he had repressed all memory of his family and early life. The questions aroused confusing feelings within him. He resolved to learn his history.

When the band returned home, the old chief gave Matthew one year to go and search for his birth parents, but he required his wife and child to stay with the tribe as security for his return.

Matthew walked from the west coast to St. Paul, Minnesota, and on to Iowa and Ohio, determined to find his family. Newspaper editors who heard about his plight wrote stories to publicize his efforts. A friend of Matthew's birth family showed them one of the articles.

William approached Matthew at a boarding house. To be certain Matthew was his brother, he asked to see if there was a scar on his foot like the one belonging to the younger Matthew. He concluded the scars were identical. There was much rejoicing at the reunion. William had always felt guilty for allowing his brother to walk to the neighbor's house alone.

Matthew met his 73-year-old father and his brothers and sisters. His mother had died shortly after he was taken captive.

After living with his family for a period of time, he enlisted with the Union's Indiana Regiment and was a brave soldier during the Civil War. He became ill at Pittsburgh Landing and died in 1862. No record was found indicating he returned to the Indian tribe.

William Walker, Sr.—adopted by Wyandotte Indians

While plowing a cornfield near Green Brier, Virginia, eleven-year-old William Walker, Sr., and his uncle were set upon by a band of roving Delawares. (30) As the pair came out of one row and started to turn down the second row, shots rang out. The uncle was hit in both arms and killed. William jumped off the plow horse and ran for the fort to sound an alarm. He never made it. Before he could reach the gate, he was hauled up on the horse of a warrior. The same group captured William's aunt.

The party then marched from Virginia to Ohio with a speed to induce suffering for the captives. The aunt and nephew were separated at the Ohio River, each going with a different group. William's group returned to Delaware, Ohio, where he had to "run the gauntlet." (31) A kind Delaware family adopted him. After about five years, the tribe attended a council in Detroit, where they met a large group of Wyandottes.

Adam Brown, an adopted white man, who was also taken from Green Brier County, recognized that William came from a family he had known in his youth. He immediately tried to open negotiations to ransom William, but the tribe and family into which William had been adopted were opposed to the exchange, on the grounds that it was against custom. They said the ties of adoption were too strong to be broken. Brown appealed to the Wyandotte chiefs. It was decided one member would address the Delaware Tribe, as a whole. The spokesman began:

> We Wyandottes are your uncles and you Delawares are
> our nephews. This you admit. Where, then, would be the
> violation of our law and custom if, all parties being
> agreed, an adopted nephew would choose to reside in the
> family of his uncle? This would be only an interchange of
> those social amenities proper among relations... (32)

The Wyandottes offered the Delawares rum and presents, not for the purchase of William, but for their continued good will. The Delawares conferred upon the arguments made and the presents offered. William was transferred the next day.

William lived with Adam Brown until he married Catharine Rankin of the Big Turtle Clan of the Wyandotte Tribe. William became a sub-agent for the Ohio Indian tribes. Under his administration, Methodism was introduced to the Wyandottes. He died in 1824.

William and Catharine's son, William, Jr., was educated at a Methodist school in Worthington, Ohio. Besides English, he learned Greek, Latin, French and five Indian languages. Three months after his father's death, he married Hannah Barrett. They had five children. The son came to be known as William Walker, Sr. He was the most influential person in the tribe. They named him head chief, while the Wyandottes still lived in Ohio. In 1831, he visited the area around Kansas City in hopes of purchasing land for the tribe to move farther west. The tribe re-located in 1843.

In 1853, the second William Walker, Sr., was named provisional governor of the Kansas/Nebraska Territory. Many other Wyandotte leading families were founded by captured and adopted white Indians. Their surnames include Hicks, Brown, Zane, Armstrong, Driver and Mudeater. (33)

Two years later, the government granted American citizenship to members of the Wyandotte Nation, but tribal lands in Kansas and Nebraska needed to be sold. The Seneca-Cayuga Tribes gave the Wyandottes 33,000 acres in north-eastern Oklahoma to replace the land that was lost.

Cynthia Ann Parker—adopted by Comanche Indians

Indian tribes sometimes massacred whole villages in their attempt to protect their way of life and the lands they held in common. (34) If the victims were not killed outright, they were kidnapped and made to work as slaves. This is what happened at Parker's Fort, Texas. Missionaries and settlers were encroaching more and more on lands that had previously been hunting grounds for the plains Indians. Hard-shell Baptist preacher Elder John Parker and his extended family built the stockade at Parker's Fort because it was far from civilization.

A large band of Comanche and Kiowa Indians raided the fort in the spring of 1836, while the white men were tending fields outside the perimeter and leaving the remainder of the group unprotected.

Cynthia Ann Parker was nine years old. Not only did she see many of her family killed, but that night she was tied up and forced to watch a scalp dance, where the Indians re-enacted their cruel deeds of violence, over and over.

Although search parties and traders looked for Cynthia Ann, she was not recognized for four years. The girl was with a band of Comanche Indians when a white trader and his Delaware Indian guide crossed her path. The men tried to ransom her, but one of the Indians, her adoptive father, told the men she would not be surrendered for any reason. When she was older, she married Comanche chief, Peta Nocona. They had several children. One of them was Quanah Parker, the fierce Comanche warrior-leader who pulled, pushed and prodded his people into the twentieth century.

Eleven years after Cynthia's first sighting, another group of white hunters spotted her. The story is that one of the men was able to get close enough to ask her if she would like to return to her people. Although she had lost her ability to speak English, she pointed to her children and shook her head, no.

In 1860, a force of United States dragoons attacked an Indian village encamped at the head of the Pease River. Cynthia and her daughter, two-year-old Prairie Flower, were captured and restored to her birth family. She had indeed lost the English language, but she responded when one of the men called her "Cynthia Ann," her birth name. She was so thoroughly Indianized that she was never comfortable in white society. When her uncle took her to Austin in 1861, she thought the assembly was one of war chiefs deciding whether she was to live or die.

Prairie Flower died in 1864 at the age of seven. Cynthia Ann died with her white family in 1870 at the age of 43. She was buried in Henderson County, Texas.

Quanah Parker never got over the loss of his mother. Although he was adopted by another Indian family, he continued to grieve for his mother. In December, 1910, her remains were moved from Texas to the Post Oak Cemetery at the Mennonite Mission in the Wichita Mountains near Lawton, Oklahoma. When Quanah died on February 23, 1911, he was buried next to her, where he had so longed to be.

These four accounts are a small sample of the surviving stories about people who were kidnapped, forced to work as slaves, and then adopted by their captors.

White Into Red by J. Norman Heard lists fifty white and Mexican captives by name who were adopted and, in varying degrees, assimilated into the Indian culture. (35) Heard believes many of the captives became more Indianized when they saw the cruelty displayed by whites in attacking unprotected Indian villages.

Other stories of Indian adoptions center on white children who purposefully ran away from their families to join the more carefree lifestyle of the Indians.

Sam Houston—adopted by Cherokee Indians

Sam Houston—that flamboyant, bigger-than-life hero of Texas—was not exactly a captured prisoner of the Indians. He ran away from his family to join the Cherokees.

After the death of Houston's father in Virginia, his family moved to Maryville, Tennessee. His brothers tried to make a farmer of him. But Sam was a reader and a dreamer. He would rather curl up under a tree with his books and let his imagination fly.

Sam hated being told what to do. So he ran away to an island called Hiawassee, at the junction of the Hiawassee River and the Big Tennessee, 50 miles from his home. He was accepted into a band of renegade Cherokee Indians, and adopted by their chief, John Jolly. (36) Sam was given the Indian name of Co-lon-neh, meaning The Raven. Indian boys taught him to play ball and he was enthralled by Cherokee mythology that he believed was comparable to stories of the Greek gods and goddesses.

Houston visited his birth mother on numerous occasions during the next three years. After much cajoling on her part about what he was going to do with his life, Houston finally opened a country school, five miles east of Maryville, Tennessee. When that closed, he joined the army, putting aside for a time the Indian life.

He distinguished himself at the Battle of Horseshoe Bend against the Creek Indians, and became a close friend of the commanding general, Andrew Jackson. During this period, he also served as a sub-agent for the Cherokees, pushing their cause in Washington, D.C. He studied law and was elected Tennessee's attorney general, then congressman, and finally, governor of Tennessee in 1827. Two years later, he married Eliza Allen. When the marriage ended three months later, Houston abruptly resigned the governorship. He settled near Fort Gibson, Indian Territory, with the Cherokees and opened a store. Some authorities believe he married Tiana Rogers, an aunt or great-aunt of Will Rogers, according to Cherokee custom. Others believe her name was Talihina. At any rate, about a year later, Houston fled for Texas, where he was made commander-in-chief of the Texas armed forces. After Houston's victory over Santa Anna, he was elected president of the Texas Republic.

He married again to Margaret Lea in 1840. Texas joined the United States in 1845 and he was elected to represent the state in the U. S. Senate. Margaret stayed in Texas raising their family of eight children, while he commuted to and from Washington, D.C. In 1859, he was elected governor of Texas, in spite of the fact that he opposed secession. At the start of the Civil War, he was thrown out of office by those who supported the Confederacy. He died two years later.

A manuscript written by Houston's son Temple recalls the theme of the Houston family: "Every tub must stand on its own bottom." (37)

Smith Paul—adopted by Chickasaw Indians

Smith Paul was sixteen years old when his mother died in North Carolina. (38) His father remarried almost immediately. A rift developed between Smith and his new step-mother, so he packed and headed west. The road took him to northwestern Mississippi, just south of Memphis. A Chickasaw Indian woman, Ela-Teecha, and her Scottish husband, Rev. A. J. McClure, adopted him. When they were moved to Oklahoma over the Trail of Tears, Paul came with them. McClure died several years later and the adopted son married his widow.

After the couple moved to Pauls Valley in southern Oklahoma in 1850, Paul returned to North Carolina several times to see his birth family, but he considered Oklahoma to be his home.

Hungry renegade Indians would pass by the Paul's home. Ela-Teecha always gave them food. She believed that if the marauding Indians had enough to eat, they would not destroy their property or take captives. The Indians respected her. No damage ever occurred on their land.

Smith Paul's son, Sam, urged Oklahoma Indians to apply for United States citizenship. He believed the government would once again take away the Indians' land, unless they were American citizens. He spent so much time away from his family that his son, Joe, nursed a bitter hatred toward him. In the end, Joe shot and killed his father.

Paul's great-grandson, Bill Paul, and his wife Cindy, authored a historical fiction novel, called *Shadow of an Indian Star* that pieces together Paul's flight from North Carolina, his adoption, and the establishment of the family in Pauls Valley, Oklahoma. (39) Three generations of Pauls set out to conquer the world. Each one—Smith, Sam, and Joe—Paul, reacted to family pressures and government policies in their own way.

Native American Indians have continued to adopt honored visitors into their respective tribes, even in the twentieth century.

John Philip Sousa—adopted by Ponca Indians

When bandleader John Philip Sousa brought his show to Ponca City, Oklahoma, in 1928, he was adopted into the Ponca Tribe in a full adoption ceremony at the 101 Ranch. (40) The ranch was owned by Sousa's personal friends, George L. Miller and his two brothers. The Millers directed the 101 Wild West Show, which played all over the United States and Europe. In Sousa's adoption ceremony, five Ponca Indian elders conferred upon him the title of chief. He was given a peace pipe and a tobacco pouch.

Eugene J. McGuinness—adopted by Osage Indians

The Osage Indian Tribe adopted Catholic Bishop Eugene J. McGuinness at a ceremony held in Pawhuska, Oklahoma, on May 17, 1947. (41) He was given the Indian name "Golden Eagle." McGuinness was a special friend of Osage Chief Fred Lookout. In addition to baptizing and confirming the elderly chief, McGuinness had prepared one hundred Native American students for the Oklahoma priesthood. The chief showed his appreciation by adopting his friend into the tribe. After Chief Lookout's death, the tribe ratified the adoption. A copy of their resolution was sent to the Bureau of Indian Affairs in April, 1950.

Our next chapter describes the ways in which white men promoted the Indian way of adoption, making it a part of mainstream society.

CHAPTER 3

FRATERNITIES

The first fraternity in the New World, established by colonists, was patterned after the League of the Iroquois. Early American patriots believed they could use the Indians' manner of dress and lifestyle to frighten and disarm the British troops. Angered by a tax on tea, the Sons of Liberty were a group of 110 Boston craftsmen and farmers, who formed their own organization, similar to a tribe and the League of the Iroquois. The Boston Tea Party was one of their first goals.

Coloring their faces with war-paint and donning Indian costumes, these "Sons of Liberty" attacked ships in the Boston Harbor, throwing all the tea on three separate ships overboard. A crewman entered the following message in the ship's log:

Between six and seven o'clock this evening came down
to the wharf a body of about one thousand people.
Among them were a number dressed and whooping like

Indians. They came on board the ships and after warning myself and the Custom-House officers to get out of the way, they unlaid the hatches and went down the hold where eighty whole and thirty-four half chests of tea, which they hoisted upon deck, and cut the chests to pieces and hove the tea all overboard, where it was damaged and lost! (42)

After the raid, the Sons of Liberty continued to agitate for freedom from the British. Most of them became soldiers and fought bravely in the Revolutionary War.

Several fraternities have descended from the Sons of Liberty and the League of the Iroquois. Thousands of Americans over the last two hundred twenty years have participated in one or more of these secret societies. People from all walks of life—from rope-makers and paperhangers to physicians, lawyers, and presidents—have been members.

Grand Order of the Iroquois

Lewis Henry Morgan, lawyer and anthropologist, joined a fraternity of young men called the Gordian Knot in Rochester, New York. (43) When the fraternity began losing members, Morgan suggested they "cut the knot." (44) They changed the name to the Grand Order of the Iroquois and adopted the Indian method of organization. Morgan hoped this would revitalize the group and make their meetings more interesting.

He served as Grand Sachem from 1844 to1846. He urged members to research Indian customs. He did much of the fieldwork himself.

Improved Order of Red Men

The Improved Order of Red Men also adopted their members. Both Theodore Roosevelt and Franklin Delano Roosevelt were "adopted" into this fraternity. The elder Roosevelt was actually adopted while he was president. The ceremony, performed by John W. Cherry, Senator A.B. Kittridge, and (Brother) Donnalley, lasted about an hour at the White House on April 17, 1906. (45) The younger Roosevelt was adopted while he was governor of New York on January 11, 1930. (46)

The only way a person could become a member of the order was through "adoption." Each prospective member or "adoptee" applied for membership in the "wigwam" through a member in good standing. Each one was investigated and, if found to be of good character, the members approved his application. During the adoption ceremony, the applicant was given more instructions as to the signs, grips and passwords he would need to enter the meeting hall and the ways to greet other members. Each candidate was given an Indian name, and was only to be addressed by that name during the meetings. (47)

"Palefaces" asked to be adopted into the order for the many social functions and charities performed by the group. The motto of the society was "freedom, friendship and charity." (48) Members were concerned about the lives of widows and orphans. When a member in good standing died, the tribe helped with the funeral expenses and sometimes performed the funeral ceremony.

Chiefs and members of local clubs from all over Illinois gathered in Springfield, the state capitol, for the 42nd Great Council Fire during the first week of October, 1919. The *Illinois State Journal,* the local daily newspaper, reported that their fire would be:

kindled in the Senate Chamber of the state house (capitol building) in hunting grounds of Springfield at the Ninth Run Rising of the Seventh Sun, Traveling Moon G.S.D. 428, which being interpreted means Tuesday morning at 9 o'clock.[sic] (49)

Pocahontas, the Illinois auxiliary to the Improved Order of Red Men, met at the same time. Their goals included supporting orphans and taking care of elderly members. Five hundred squaws participated in three council fires from the Springfield area alone. Tongue in cheek, a reporter wrote, "Legislation will be passed for the benefit of local councils in the state…there will be a heap much business." (50)

Masonry

Masons also "adopted" new members into their fraternity, much like the Indians adopted visitors into their campsites to honor them.

The three tenets of masonry are brotherly love, relief and truth. They teach that the whole human race is one family and that the individual is created by "one Almighty Parent." The duty of masons is to relieve the misery of unfortunate individuals and to regulate their own conduct by the principle of truth. (51)

A handbook for Oklahoma masons called *Murrow's Masonic Monitor* quotes the presiding mason's remarks to all newly inducted members

We hope that you will cultivate a warm attachment to that family of love into which you are now adopted, the pleasures and advantages of which you are beginning to realize…our good opinion of you induced us to receive with pleasure your application…into our society. (52)

Female relatives of masons were also adopted into a separate secret society. Albert Pike's *Masonry of Adoption: Masonic Rituals for Women* describes three rituals for women who are being inducted into the society. The first three degrees which the pledges earn through study are called apprentice, companion and mistress. During the ritual to become an apprentice, the leader asks the new member if she is an Apprentice Masoness of Adoption. The applicant is to answer affirmatively. Then the leader asks, "Where were you adopted an Apprentice?" She answers, "In the bosom of the lodge." (53)

The leader concludes the ritual with one last question.

Are you willing to assume a solemn obligation, which…will bind you an apprentice to virtue…and to the performance of all duties that can devolve on woman as Daughter of her Parents and of the State? (54)

The second ritual recounts the story of the first parents Adam and Eve. Women who are studying for the degree of Companion are exhorted to put away all selfishness and aspire to become a person benefiting humanity.

During the applicant's study for the third degree of Mistress, she is taught the meaning of the story of Moses and his adoption by Pharaoh's daughter. Moses' mother is expected to feel gratified that she can receive wages for taking care of her son, while the princess is the adoptive mother.

The leader then asks the new member how the lodge works. She is expected to say, "Because the Rite of Adoption reflects the Light of Freemasonry, as the Moon does that of the Sun." (55)

Cosmos Club

John Wesley Powell, the director of the U. S. Geological Survey and the Bureau of Indian Ethnology, formed the Cosmos Club in 1878 as an elite men's club in Washington, D.C. The original purpose of the group was to discuss current events and ways to improve society by using scientific principles. While the basic organization of the club wasn't a fraternity, the philosophy of some of its members lends itself to this discussion. The members met weekly in Washington, D.C., to promote their goals.

In addition to Powell, Lester Frank Ward, the author of the first American sociology text, was a charter member of the Cosmos Club.

Ward's childhood experience was harsh. Born to wandering parents, he began to support himself by working in the mills at age eleven. He also worked on a farm to earn money for school. Ward's parents and other family members were indifferent to his prospects in life. He had to pay all of his own board, room, and school expenses. He married and passed the test to become a public school teacher. He was fired from his first teaching position, because the parents were upset with his concern for discipline.

When President Lincoln called for recruits for the Union Army, Ward enlisted. He was wounded three times at Chancellorsville. After his medical discharge, Ward knocked on many doors seeking employment. He was finally hired as a temporary clerk in the U. S. Treasury Department. Two years later, he transferred to the Bureau of Statistics. By attending night school, he earned a B.A. degree in 1869. Two years later, he earned a law degree. He received a master's degree and a medical diploma in 1872.

Ward was impressed by many of the great writers: Auguste

Comte, Herbert Spencer, John Stuart Mill, and others. He began formulating his ideas in a manuscript to be called *Dynamic Sociology.*

In Ward's first magazine article, entitled "The Local Distribution of Plants and the Theory of Adaptation," Ward said that individuals are not perfectly adapted to their environments. His biographer, Alvin Nelson, described the author's unusual perspective:

> He pointed out cases of plants that grew more vigorously when introduced into a country different from that in which they originated, and that many plants flourish better under cultivation than in a natural state....The thesis that individuals may prosper better under care and protection than under natural conditions became one of the important bases of his melioristic social theories. (56, 57)

Samuel Chugerman described Ward's viewpoint of evolution as moving from God to nature and then to man.

> Heredity has been overstressed, while environmental influences have been incredibly neglected. By a sane balance of the two, education and not "blood" will tell, for education is the most powerful factor in social evolution. (58)

Chugerman added that Ward believed man must use his intellect to beat nature, by improving upon her methods. "That can be done only by recognizing the existence of a social mind and giving it the reins of social control..." (59)

Ward believed our society could be modeled after the natural sciences (mind over matter, or mind "fixing" the mistakes of nature), and he worked diligently to achieve that goal.

In 1881 Ward transferred from the Bureau of Statistics to Powell's U. S. Geological Survey. At night he continued to write about his social theories. When Ward was unable to find a publisher, Powell put him in touch with D. Appleton and Company. A contract was worked out and the manuscript became a small press run. In addition to *Dynamic Sociology*, Ward authored *Pure Sociology, Applied Sociology, Glimpses of the Cosmos, and Psychic Factors of Civilization.*

Throughout his life, Ward continued to push for public education and the ability of the state to use scientific methods to help people through "social engineering."

Ward believed neither nature nor society had been arranged for the benefit of human beings or other creatures.

Nature is in fact badly designed. Bark grows too tightly on trees, constricting their growth. Insects foolishly die in stinging their attackers. Moths fly stupidly into flames. A cod lays a million eggs a year in order that two may survive. An eel carries around nine million eggs simply to reproduce itself. The mother opossum gives birth to more babies than she has teats for feeding…Rational man must assume "the attitude of a master or ruler" over the whole continent, subjugating nature's energies to her own ends. Inefficiency must give way to efficiency, *laissez-faire* to intelligent planning, self-interest to the common good …the human mind must take over the management of all evolution. (60)

Ward seemed to believe that the government should fix all mistakes of nature and of society. He continued to work for the U. S. Geological Service until his retirement in 1906, when Brown University appointed him professor of sociology. He remained in that post until his death in 1913.

Long before Ward put pen to paper in developing his theory of sociology and social justice, a New England minister began to act on his personal idea of charity and theology—by shipping thousands of New York City's street children to the Midwest.

Chapter 4 details that story.

CHAPTER 4

THE ORPHAN TRAIN

Reverend Charles Loring Brace was a man with a mission. Every day, rain or shine, hot or cold, energetic or fatigued, he scoured New York City for children. He looked on street corners, under bridges, in brothels, around pool halls and landfills—anywhere young people might be loitering or scavenging for a living.

Crowds of children thronged around him to listen to his wonderful stories of a future in the West. Cowboys and Indians, campfires and chuck wagons, fields of golden grain and lucrative jobs in agriculture fired their imaginations.

Brace's friends believed he was doing God's work—educating vagrant street children for meaningful careers. His critics charged he sold children into slavery and encouraged runaways. Based on the available historical evidence, these two opposing views may never be resolved.

What we do know, however, is that Brace's Orphan Train removed 130,000 children from America's largest city to farmers' homes in the West and Midwest between 1854 and 1929. (61) Some received good homes. Others did not.

Brace referred to the Orphan Train program as "Emigration." It began when Reverend Brace and other businessmen created an organization called the Children's Aid Society to educate New York City's vagrant street children for the job market.

The first meeting of the society was held in February, 1853. The following announcement was placed in the *New York Daily Times* on March 3, 1853:

> We have formed an association, which shall devote itself entirely to this class of vagrant children. We do not propose in any way to conflict with existing Asylums and Institutions, but to render them a hearty cooperation, and, at the same time, to fill a gap, which of necessity, they have all left. A large multitude of children live in the city, which cannot be placed in Asylums, and yet who are uncared for and ignorant and vagrant. We propose to give these work; and to bring them under religious influence. (62)

Brace was appointed secretary of the group. They established industrial schools to train boys for work. Children were matched with the available jobs in the city. When the need for work outstripped the number of positions, they looked toward the West for new job opportunities. Farmers, churches, and business leaders were contacted in hopes they would supply jobs for the youth of New York City. Brace believed the children could be moved out of the urban setting and trained for a lifetime of industry and hard work.

Farmers jumped at the chance for almost free work with little chance of being investigated for child labor violations because most states had not yet passed child labor laws.

The first children were "placed out" in 1854. That term came from the Orphan Train experience itself. When the train pulled into a rural depot, the children were "placed out" on the platform for the townspeople to look over and choose which children they would like to take home.

Editors for *The New York Herald* were not cheerleaders of the Children's Aid Society. In 1874, they ran a series of stories about all of the relief organizations in New York City. Most of the charities cooperated with the newspaper and sent copies of their financial reports for the editors to print. The Children's Aid Society did not.

A scathing newspaper article about the society appeared on February 22, 1874. They published a letter written by the brother of an orphan train rider. He charged that Brace seduced his brother into riding the train in spite of the fact that he was employed and had a large, extended family in the city. Letters from the brother indicated he spent long hours in the farmer's fields and there was not enough to eat. He returned home after their father sent him money for the train ride home. Brace tried to "place out" the young man a second time, even after he had returned to the city. (63)

Here is a fictional conversation with Reverend Brace, as if a present-day television journalist was interviewing him. The answers are based on *The Life of Charles Loring Brace*, written by his sister Emma Brace.

*　　*　　*

A MODERN TELEVISION JOURNALIST

INTERVIEWS REV. CHARLES LORING BRACE,

FOUNDER OF THE ORPHAN TRAIN MOVEMENT (64)

JOURNALIST: "Thank you for joining us, Reverend Brace. Please sit down."

BRACE: "It's a pleasure to be here. I always enjoy talking about the programs we have within the Children's Aid Society."

JOURNALIST (To the audience): "Charles Loring Brace was born June 19, 1826, in Litchfield, Connecticut. His ancestors were Puritans. His father, John Brace, was principal of the Female Seminary in Hartford, Connecticut. The younger Brace is currently a noted columnist and head of New York City's Children's Aid Society."

JOURNALIST: "Reverend Brace, you were trained as a minister, but you're not preaching. Is that right?"

BRACE: "Yes, the craft of being a real minister is passing away. You have to have people in the sanctuary listening to you in order to be effective. Our newspapers are our pulpits now."

JOURNALIST: "So that's why you write for several papers in the New England area?"

BRACE: "Yes, I want to have a worthwhile impact on the lives of people—children and adults. I want to cure poverty and misery."

JOURNALIST: "In one of your columns, you criticized New York City's soup kitchens. What do you have against soup?"

BRACE: "I always enjoy good soup, but the soup kitchens are misguided charity. It's giving the poor something they haven't earned. It won't make them better citizens."

JOURNALIST: "Reverend Brace, have you worked for everything you have ever had?"

BRACE "Yes, of course."

JOURNALIST: "And what work did you do when you were a child?"

BRACE: "Why, I was a student."

JOURNALIST: "Were you at a boarding school?"

BRACE: "No, my father was a teacher and he taught me."

JOURNALIST: "I understand your mother died when you were fourteen. Was your mother important in your life?"

BRACE: "I loved my mother. But I spent most of my time with father."

JOURNALIST: "Where would you have been if your father had not been a teacher?"

BRACE: "I don't know."

JOURNALIST: "If your father had had a factory job, wouldn't you have been roaming the streets?"

BRACE: "I can't speculate on that. I have always loved books. I spent hours and hours studying Latin, history, and philosophy."

JOURNALIST: "So you didn't spend a lot of time learning the games that children play?"

BRACE: "No, my father and I walked. He lectured while we walked and then I wrote up my notes the next day, in addition to all the reading I was doing. Sometimes, I had to write the notes over and over, until I was able to clarify in written form what he had given to me verbally. Then he would have me read to him. He was a master of elocution. He was always very critical of my ability to read aloud."

JOURNALIST: "What kinds of things did you read?"

BRACE: "I read Shakespeare, Homer, Plato, Aristotle, and many of the Greek myths."

JOURNALIST: "Did you resent this kind of training?"

BRACE: "My mother wasn't well, and I knew that if I wanted to stay with my father, then I had to submit to the schooling. I did enjoy learning."

JOURNALIST: "You applied yourself so you could stay with your father?"

BRACE: "Yes, I did."

JOURNALIST: "What about this emigration program?"

BRACE: "As Horace Greeley was fond of saying, 'Go West, young man.' (65) We are giving the street children of New York an opportunity to have their own Manifest Destiny in the West. The farmer's home is a wonderful educational institution. The farmers are all good people who need help with their farm chores. They will teach these children the value of work. They will earn their board and room by the work that they do. The farmers are crying for us to send them more children."

JOURNALIST: "Where did this idea come from?"

BRACE: "New York City has too many street children—children with no home, or with parents who are too dumb to take care of them. Many are living in tenements without running water. They only wash once a week at a public bathhouse. These children will turn to crime if they aren't catapulted into a moral environment— the family farm. The farmers are begging for more farm labor. It's economy—you put the supply with the demand."

JOURNALIST: "You don't like these children's parents, do you?"

BRACE: "They aren't moral people themselves, so how can they help their children to grow up to be happy, productive citizens?"

JOURNALIST: "There have been charges that you sell the children into slavery."

BRACE: "We only give assistance. We want to discourage pauperism and help build character. These are poor children 'implanted by Christianity' in the West, much like seeds are sown in more productive soil where they are capable of growth. Jesus talked about planting seeds in good ground in the Gospel of Mark–chapter four, verse eight." (66)

JOURNALIST: "How can you be certain these children won't be abused in their new homes?"

BRACE: "There are millions of acres of land to the West. These are American farmers. The children won't be abused. The farmers need them for work. They won't go hungry. And they won't end up in prison."

JOURNALIST: "What propelled you into beginning this plan?"

BRACE: "Well, there is a group of people who believe these children should be housed in asylums, but the children can't legally be committed, because they haven't done anything wrong. Changing their environment will help to educate the children better than anything else."

JOURNALIST: "So why do you think all these children are going to prison?"

BRACE: "No human power can save these children if they are left in their own surroundings." (67)

JOURNALIST: "Have you been a victim of crime in New York City?"

BRACE: "No."

JOURNALIST: "But you were in prison in Hungary?"

BRACE: "Yes. As a young man, I hitchhiked all over Europe, studying each country's history, religion, and economic system. I was paid for newspaper columns that I sent back to the states for publication. I was falsely arrested in Hungary. This was just after the Hungarian Rebellion of 1848. The police accused me of writing revolutionary material. I was imprisoned for a month, with no way of communicating with the outside world. A friend secured my release. Being in prison was a horrible experience. My mind chafed at the loss of freedom. The absurdity of the charges made it even worse."

JOURNALIST: "So, in your mind, these children have a choice. They can leave their birth parents and emigrate or they can go to prison. Is that right?"

BRACE: (His face turns red. He grabs the arm of the chair and his upper body lunges forward.) "How dare you criticize the life I have chosen for each child? I'm working hard for God. We're making these children worthwhile, contributing members of society. They didn't have anything before they went west. Their parents were filthy. They weren't being educated for any meaningful work. We want to reduce crime in New York City. We don't want to have to pay to build any more prison cells. It costs only $15 to send a child west. It costs $150 to keep the same child in an asylum for a year."

JOURNALIST: "So it all comes down to money."

BRACE: "These children are better off living outside of New York City—no matter what you say."

JOURNALIST: "Thank you for joining us with your views, Reverend Brace. Good night, America."

*   *   *

A record of Brace's preoccupation with the lack of moral character in the children and parents of New York City has been left in his columns and books.

His first column in the *New York Daily Times*, titled "Walks Among the New York Poor" described his tour of New York City with a missionary, known only as Mr. Pease. The gentleman introduced Brace to a young woman who was employed in a garment factory for a few pennies per day.

When Brace asked him what would happen to her, Pease replied that many young women like her come to an end in the brothel or in a venereal disease hospital.

Brace wrote, "God help them say I, from my heart, for man seldom will." (68)

The article does not include any information about children, but four months later the Children's Aid Society was formed.

The most readily available record of Brace's thoughts on children was published in his book, *The Dangerous Classes of New York and Twenty Years' Work Among Them*. He began by detailing the terrible treatment of children in Greek and Roman societies:

> When one thinks what was the fate of one large and pitiable class of human beings—unfortunate children, destitute orphans, foundlings, the deformed and sickly, and female children of the poor….how universal… infanticide was; how Plato and Aristotle approved of it; how even more common was the dreadful exposure of children who were physically imperfect or for any cause disagreeable to their parents, so that crowds of these little unfortunates were to be seen exposed around a column in Rome—some being taken to be raised as slaves, others as prostitutes, others carried off by beggars and maimed for exhibition or captured by witches to be murdered…when one remembers for how many centuries, even after the nominal introduction of Christianity, the sale of free children was permitted by law and then recalls how Christianity has exterminated these barbarous practices… purified the morals, raised the character and made happy the life of foundlings. (69)

Then he recounts numerous tales of the decadence of New York City's youth. It would seem that the evils of slavery, prostitution and infanticide were not far from the minds of early emigration and adoption advocates.

"The Boy Who Went Wrong" is the title of an article in *The Century Magazine*, which was designed to show how different environments may affect an individual's behavior. Author H.

Addison Bruce wrote an incredible tale from a memory he had about two boys who stole apples. One was caught and went to jail. The other escaped and returned to his loving home. Later in life, the boy who was exposed to the criminal element in jail commits murder. He is brought before a judge, the same person who helped him steal apples! Bruce wrote that the positive environment had prevented the judge from continuing a life of crime. His next example was from the famous Juke family. Seven hundred family members were studied for their low educational performance, prostitution and other criminal behavior. One child, however, was placed in an adoptive home with loving parents. According to Bruce, he became an exemplary citizen. (70)

Records of the Orphan Train riders have been difficult to retrieve, partly because many people believe adoptees have no right to their history, and also because record-keeping was scant.

The National Orphan Train Museum, based in Concordia, Kansas, is seeking memorabilia and soliciting stories of train riders—our pioneer "adoptees."

In our next chapter we will turn our attention to organizations whose members advocated sexual purity and for the suppression of prostitution, as well as placing children in adoptive homes.

CHAPTER 5

THE NEW ABOLITIONISTS

While Charles Loring Brace was removing children and teenagers from parents he considered to be immoral, other nineteenth-century reformers were encouraging temperance, working to ban prostitution and promoting two parent families.

Adoption history is linked to these kinds of individual and societal attitudes, developed within voluntary agencies and groups.

Like the buried cables of your telephone, like the indirect influence of the textbook publisher, the services of the American Social Hygiene Association (ASHA) may or may not be seen, but they are not any the less necessary and valuable to your health and future welfare. They help you build a better place for your children to grow up in. (71)

Neither the national purity movement nor the subsequent ASHA actively promoted adoption, but some members used their journal and other literature to indirectly press for adoption.

Let's journey back in time to the mid-1800s. Abolition writers, shocked by the cruelties slavery imposed upon black Americans, churned out thousands of words against the system during the first half of the nineteenth century. Their articles and editorials appeared in newspapers and magazines across the land. These journalists saw their words ignite the Civil War and snuff out the system they felt was depriving their black brothers and sisters of individual liberty.

The signing of the Emancipation Proclamation in 1863 and Lee's surrender at Appomattox in 1865 climaxed years of written attacks upon the institution of slavery.

As the Civil War drew to a close, abolition writers looked for other issues to arouse their readers. They didn't have to look far. The journalists began to pour their energies into the fight to stop prostitution in America, which they equated with the slavery of women. They were social feminists who believed in a system of values, elevating women to the same standard as men.

Richard Pivar described these new abolitionists as

dedicated to the emancipation of the white slave—the prostitute. Their immediate objectives of eradicating prostitution and ending the white slave traffic expanded tremendously, however, once they actually encountered the institution and its 'fallen women.' Preventive social reforms based on child-rearing and education became their broader objective. While they retained a negative goal—eradication of sin and evil—they added a positive goal—the reconstruction of American society through its children. (72)

These advocates of social purity fought city ordinances, which allowed the licensing of brothels. The Women's Christian Temperance Union (WCTU) established a whole department dedicated to social purity. Alcohol and sex were seen as twin evils, because many brothels were attached to taverns.

In addition to the WCTU, religious leaders of all faiths and reformers from all walks of life supported the idea of social purity—that man could and should be taught to be "perfect," at least in the eyes of his fellow man. This "perfectibility" was seen as moral education in the areas of sex education, intemperance, pornography, diet, dress and personal cleanliness. Prostitution became the first target of the social purists' wrath, because it was believed to be an enemy of the family. In their eyes, the nuclear family was the best way for society to pass along the skills necessary for individuals to develop into worthwhile citizens.

Fearing what urban life might be like without the family to teach moral standards to its children, social purity activists lobbied state legislatures and municipal leaders to ban prostitution and to raise the age of consent for girls.

Abby Hopper Gibbons, a Quaker reformer, led New York City's branch of the National Social Purity Alliance (NSPA). She distributed social purity programs and ideas to every reform agency in New York City. As the president of the New York Women's Prison Association, Gibbons must have counseled with Charles Loring Brace, the head of the Children's Aid Society, and founder of the Orphan Train. When Brace visited Boston, he wrote to Gibbons, extolling the virtues of her son, who was a student in Boston at the time. (73)

Gibbons was also editor of the official journal for the NSPA. In May, 1894, *The Philanthropist* published an article by Philadelphia reformer Mrs. E. S. Turner, in which she publicized the work of a group of women who found foster and adoptive homes for babies in foundling hospitals. It may have been one of the first adoption agencies:

> There has lately been established in Philadelphia an association which aims to be an improvement on the old-time foundling hospital. Instead of a great building in which are congregated all the infants of whom their mothers are ashamed, there is a directory of women, chosen not only for their tenderness, but also for their experience and wisdom; these women found no new institution, but aim to establish relations with all existing institutions interested in poor or deserted children, and supply them with means for a further extension of their work. The advantages of such a system over the traditional foundling are these: For some cause, not very well understood, whenever very young creatures, whether lambs, calves, or babies, are herded together, they pine and die; this is the case in hospitals where cleanliness and reasonable care are observed. The Directory proposes to board all infants in the country when practicable, or at any rate in private families, keeping a systematic oversight of their treatment. (74)

Mrs. Turner said the women would encourage each birth mother to keep her child and to find employment.

> If circumstances don't permit this, or if the disgrace is more than the unfortunate girl can bear, they will keep her secret and help her in all ways to regain her self-respect, at the same time preserving for her such traces of her child that if, at any time, she should be strong enough to claim it, she may have the power. (75)

The purpose of this system was to give the birth mother an opportunity to experience some maternal feelings, before "flinging the babe into oblivion, relieved from ever seeing or hearing from it again." (76)

In October, 1895, the NSPA held a three-day conference in Baltimore, Maryland, called the National Purity Congress. During the convention, sixty leaders of the purity movement delivered lectures to the membership. Aaron M. Powell, president of the Alliance, saved their words in book form, entitled *The National Purity Congress, Its Papers, Addresses and Portraits.*

Mrs. Isabel Lake of Chicago suggested building a home, to be called "The Nest," for babies.

While the unwavering principle must be to keep mother and baby together, still many will come under our care that need our efforts, that may benefit the homeless child and the childless home. (77)

Rev. A. H. Lewis made a point against parents who might be intemperate. He said that "whatever impairs a perfected physical life, also makes a man unfit for fatherhood." (78) A similar assertion in that time frame could have been made for women— those who were intemperate were seen by many as being unfit for motherhood.

In the period following this congress, many local daily and weekly papers carried articles and editorials, inciting readers toward the social purity ethic and banning prostitution.

Justice, a weekly socialist paper in southwestern Oklahoma, ran several articles about white slavery. One article, entitled "Only a Working Girl," suggested prostitution was caused by hiring girls to work in factories at less than a living wage.

We ask you, dear reader, what can this girl do when her wages won't even pay her board, let alone clothing and other necessities of life. She will choose the life of a prostitute in preference to starvation. (79)

On May 31, 1907, *Justice* reprinted an editorial from the Peoria, Illinois, *Socialist*, which reported the Crittenton Mission of New York estimated 300,000 women and girls in the United States were living in brothels. "Is your daughter's future absolutely secure?" the article asked. "Are you content for your neighbor's daughter to be any less secure?" (80)

They added a patriotic note to the cause of freedom from white slavery with a poem, entitled, 'White Slaves of America:' "Go light the beacon fires that flashed on Bunker Hill and quench them not till Mammon's flag trails low." (81, 82)

Several downtown brothels served Oklahoma City at the turn of the century. In 1910, Mrs. Nora M. Pearl, a former Oklahoma City police matron and editor of Oklahoma's WCTU newsletter, formed a Traveler's Aid Society. She posted matrons in three railroad stations to meet every train, so women would not be lured into rooming houses which turned out to be brothels. Girls were helped with appropriate lodging, and employment was secured for them, if necessary. Mrs. Pearl also cared for dependent children. In October, 1910, *The Daily Oklahoman* carried two articles about children who were available for adoption through the Traveler's Aid Society. (83)

Oklahoma was one of the first states to pass an anti-white slavery law. (84) In late 1910, Congress passed the Mann-Elkins Act, which made it a federal crime to transport a woman across a state line for an immoral purpose.

As many of the older NSPA members retired or passed away, the torch of the movement passed to three organizations: the American Vigilance Association, the American Federation for Sex Hygiene and the Bureau of Social Hygiene.

The American Vigilance Association's official journal, entitled *Vigilance*, carried several articles, which touched on illegitimacy and adoption. They reprinted a speech given by Mrs. Jessie Hodder of the Massachusetts General Hospital to the Conference on Child Welfare at Clark University in July, 1909. While she did not advocate adopting out every baby born to unmarried parents, she remarked

> Society is coming more and more to recognize itself as over-parent, and should demand that every child in a natural home shall be reared as a good citizen. In these illegitimate children, with only half a home to start with, it is a clear duty to enforce this standard; and just crudely to leave every illegitimate child with its mother, good or bad, capable or incapable, devoted or criminally careless, would be a wrong to many children and to the State. (85)

In June, 1912, *Vigilance* published its first article on eugenics, the science of heredity and being well-born. The author, David Starr Jordan, said that breeding better men would make a better society, and that even well-born children could be ruined by coming into contact with slums and red-light districts.

"To have good men and women, we must have good parents from which they may spring," Jordan wrote. (86)

In August of the same year, *Vigilance* ran an editorial about a conference of social workers, where the question of which babies were to be separated from their unmarried mothers was discussed.

The editor wrote, "It was readily agreed that a normal mother should keep her child, and a feeble-minded mother should not." (87)

In the last issue of *Vigilance*, an article, entitled "The Myth of the Educated Prostitute," appeared. It clarified their view of the educational status of prostitutes.

Many investigators testified that a large proportion of prostitutes are mentally inferior...It may be accepted as fundamental to the right understanding of prostitution that a prevalent factor in the problem is the mental deficiency of the prostitute. (88)

S. W. Dickinson, superintendent of the Children's Home Society of Minnesota, sent a letter to *Vigilance* about the fate of children born to unmarried parents.

In a number of cases, the mother abandons the child by leaving it in some cheap boarding place and is never heard from again. Such a child must come before the court for disposition, and through an order of commitment to an institution attains a legal status and can be placed in a family home where its future standing is permanently secured...I believe that, if the fact of parentage was fully known and recorded through court proceedings, there would be a wholesome, deterrent moral influence. (89)

In 1914, John D. Rockefeller, Jr., provided the funding to merge the three major purity organizations, forming the American Social Hygiene Association (ASHA). The term 'social hygiene' was chosen as a more acceptable name than terms such as purity, sex, or prophylaxis.

William Freeman Snow, M.D., a public health professor at

Stanford University, was elected the association's first secretary. He worked with Harvard Professor Charles William Eliot to make ASHA a national organization, fighting for the suppression of prostitution and opening society to a discussion of venereal disease and sex hygiene. ASHA's first thrust was to study the problem in depth. Abraham Flexner was commissioned to continue his study of the white slave laws and police administrations in Europe. George J. Kneeland studied vice in New York City.

Both Snow and Eliot were tireless workers in the movement. Eliot later became president of Harvard University. Other educators were also part of ASHA.

Reverend Leland Foster Wood was Professor of Social Ethics at Colgate-Rochester Divinity School. He later became secretary of the Committee on Marriage and Family. He wrote much of the ASHA manual, which was used by ministers from almost every religion to counsel young people across America on sex education.

Anna Garlin Spencer, associate director of the New York School of Social Work and professor of sociology and ethics in the Meadville Theological School, was also part of ASHA. When she taught a class on Problems in Family Life at Columbia University, Mrs. Spencer's syllabus included such topical questions as "Have Unmarried Women a Social Right to Motherhood?" and "What is the real problem of illegitimate children?" (90)

ASHA's answer to that question may have been in a book review of *The Practicable Ideal of Protection and Care for Children Born Out of Wedlock* by Rev. Robert F. Keegan, secretary for charities to the Archbishop of New York, reprinted from the *Catholic Charities Review*. Keegan wrote, "The community must see that the parents do not evade their responsibilities. It must protect itself from imposition." (91)

Even in 1921, many citizens were loath to spend dollars on children and child care. Others were more liberal.

The matter of money can be arranged, but the matter of the home and care of two parents is still impossible to adjust. The child has a right to be born in the best circumstances society can give him and to that respect for both parents which only the knowledge that they have ranged themselves on the side of right living can give. (92)

ASHA members believed that only a moral, nuclear family could fulfill the duties involved with the rearing of children.

Another Catholic priest, Reverend William J. Gibbons, wrote

Unstable families and loose attitudes toward family stability inevitably bring in their wake sexual aberrations, which harm society. Mental and physical diseases, of varying degrees of intensity, accompany family collapse and the promiscuity usually associated with such collapse...The family is not merely a social institution; it is an institution regulated by natural law. Its monogamous character, its stability and permanence, its relationship to the education and rearing of children all have profound social significance. But these functions have a deeper origin than social utility; they are in accord with the divine plan of society. (93)

Our next chapter describes the child saving movement, which began to develop a "divine plan" for children.

CHAPTER 6

CHICAGO CHILD SAVING

Chicago, sprawling metropolis of the Midwest, became home to thousands of immigrants in the 1800s. Its factories and meat packing plants absorbed the labor of many unskilled men and women. Their families were incidental to the employment process. Parents had to work, so young children fended for themselves. As in New York, they roamed the streets, picking up coal along the railroad tracks for their stoves and, when necessary, digging in the trash to fill their bellies.

In May of 1898, a three-year-old Chinese girl was reported to have fallen into the Chicago River at Harrison Street. A compassionate passerby plucked her from certain drowning. The child cried in Chinese for her mother. The wailing continued at the police station. The *Chicago Evening Journal* reported that "applicants" for the small Chinese girl should be referred to the Harrison Street Annex. (94) The advertisement was aimed at finding foster parents for the child, not her biological parents.

Perhaps officials looked for the parents, but it seemed as if they didn't care whether she was reunited with her birth parents or not.

Children in America have not always been valued and protected. Framers of the United States' Constitution ignored children's issues. State constitutions treated wives and kids like chattel.

A child might not come to the attention of the authorities unless he or she did something for which the young person could be arrested, tried, convicted, and put in prison with adult offenders. No distinction was made between juvenile and adult criminals.

While Charles L. Brace's method of removing children by the rail car load from the crowded city to rural areas may have been outlandish and careless, it was the spark of an idea that called for sacrifice on the part of thousands of children, to move society toward establishing a workable system of child welfare and adoption.

The first Chicago child saver was Martin Van Arsdale, a young preacher from Green Valley, Illinois, who had a heart for children. He believed he could fine-tune Brace's plan by placing one child at a time. When a homeless or neglected child came into his care, he and his wife Isabelle made every effort to place the juvenile with an appropriate family. The couple worked long and hard hours. The project was more than the couple could handle on their own.

They established the Illinois Children's Home and Aid Society in 1883. (95) Advisory boards in each community located children needing assistance and made inquiries for prospective adoptive parents. Funds were raised through voluntary contributions.

The headquarters moved to Chicago in 1884. When the organization expanded into other states, it became known as the

National Children's Home Society. The second state to establish its own society was Iowa. In 1886, Van Arsdale spoke at a church in Clinton, Iowa, where Edward P. Savage was pastor. His mind was a fertile field for Van Arsdale's idea.

When Savage accepted a pastorate in St. Paul, he immediately began making contacts to establish a similar society in Minnesota. On September 11, 1889, Savage was named superintendent of the new Minnesota Children's Home Society. (96) He organized local advisory boards, but he felt his main task was to place children. He spent huge chunks of time on the road, picking up and delivering children to all parts of Minnesota. LeRoy Ashby, author of *Saving the Waifs*, noted that Savage may have been lackadaisical in placing children, because he depended on his own personal contacts to make placements. The society did not require references from prospective adoptive parents in its early years. (97)

As the Home Societies began to flourish, other youth-oriented groups gained ground, too.

Timothy D. Hurley, a young Chicago lawyer who served as president of the Catholic Visitation and Aid Society, urged 1891 Illinois legislators to pass a juvenile court bill, which would allow judges to handle children's cases separately from the criminal court. The idea was defeated.

In 1893, Illinois governor John P. Atgeld appointed Julia C. Lathrop, the daughter of former Congressman William Lathrop, to be the first woman member of the State Board of Charities. (98) She immediately began to personally inspect every jail and poor house in Illinois, including all places where children were housed. She was appalled at the conditions. "Young children were shut up with the most depraved adults and being trained in crime, instead of being kept away from it." (99) Lathrop believed the experience would so damage the young people that they could not become good citizens. She and other commission members began working in the background to renew efforts for a juvenile court, which would protect minors from the adult criminal court.

Lathrop was an astute politician. She believed the issue should not go to the legislature as a woman's measure, if it was going to pass. "We must get the bar association involved." (100)

The Illinois Bar Association appointed a committee to address the issue. Judge Harvey B. Hurd, along with Ephraim Banning and Hurley, worked industriously to write the legislation and lobby the legislature for its passage.

The juvenile court bill became law in Illinois on April 14, 1899. Supporters were ecstatic. Reality, however, exacted a lot of hard work! While it was true that the legislature approved of the juvenile court, they did not provide any funding to implement the law. No additional housing space was provided.

Judge Richard S. Tuthill was appointed to be the first juvenile judge. (101) Social worker Lucy L. Flower suggested using volunteer probation officers. (102) Women's groups actually donated funds to pay for some probation services for children. Other women donated their time. Many church ladies took turns being in the children's court, taking notes. Without supervision, they would investigate the child's home life and report back to the judge. His options were limited, because of lack of space in the existing juvenile facilities. He could commit a child to any institution in the state that was authorized to house children. Or, he could send the child home to be with his parents, requiring the juvenile to have the services of a probation officer. Another choice was to remove the child from his natural home and send him or her to live with the few available foster families, while continuing to make adjustments with the birth family, in hopes of reuniting the child with his parents. The juvenile court judge was expected to have the wisdom of Solomon. While everyone wanted what was best for each child, the decisions were based on what was economically feasible and on the subjective information gathered by homemakers, whose hobby was child saving!

Volunteers scrambled to find foster homes for the many delinquent and dependent children who came to the attention of the court. When there weren't enough foster families to go around, children were sent to faith-based, sectarian societies for care. These institutions soon bulged with more children than they could adequately house.

As president of the Visitation and Aid Society, Hurley continued to gather community resources for the juvenile court. He edited a monthly journal, called *The Juvenile Court Record*, which helped publicize the good work child savers were doing in Chicago. (103) The journal was distributed all over the United States. Its first goal was to encourage every state to have a juvenile court.

In January, 1904, Hurley published the remarks of Hastings H. Hart, who extolled the virtues of adoption for dependent children. Hart said he believed it was necessary to place children now in institutions into adoptive homes, making room for other dependent children to take their place. Hart pointed to the good work in the State of Minnesota, which had not built a new orphan asylum for 15 years, because they were placing children in family homes. (104)

In the same issue, Hurley posted the following comments in his editorial:

Our doctrine has ever been to keep children out of the court, if possible. We have insisted from the first that home was the proper place for a child. If the home was not what it ought to be, then influence should be brought to bear on it that would make it a fit place in which to rear children. By all means whenever possible, the family should be kept together. If the task of uplifting the family proves too great a one to be mastered, then the child should be placed in a good home. We believe there are enough childless homes in this country for every homeless child. (105)

In September, 1904, Sherman C. Kingsley, general superintendent of the Chicago Relief and Aid Society, spoke at the annual conference of the National Children's Home Society. He remarked that one man had placed 500 children in family homes over a large state. He didn't see how one individual could adequately supervise such a tremendous workload. "It's like livestock or a world's fair exhibit…it's our business to know whether a child has gone to happiness or a wretched exile… there is no excuse for blundering!" (106) He did not name the individual. There is no way of ascertaining to whom he was referring.

However, in 1908, Minnesota's Edward P. Savage came under fire for his child-placing practices. Three co-workers complained to the society's board that, among other things, children were being lost, because there was no follow-up after placement. They also said Savage accepted sick and malnourished babies, which he placed in family homes.

The Board opened an investigation. Charges and counter-charges flew back and forth. While the board refused to affirm the charges, they did find Savage's management style promoted ill feeling among the workers. He was removed as superintendent, but he continued to work for the society until his death. During his 20 years as superintendent, 2,500 children were placed in family homes. (107) Ashby reported that half of those children were returned and then placed a second time. Some children continued to float from home to home.

The board appointed Reverend Samuel W. Dickinson to replace Savage as superintendent. He was interested in standardizing placement and becoming more scientific in all aspects of child saving work. He believed that if more care was taken in preparation for the initial placement, then it was less likely the children would be returned.

Ashby wrote that Dickinson had told his board that one-third of the adoptive parent applications had to be rejected. "It requires courage to deny people who may be kind, love children, but whose conditions of home life are not suitable." (108)

Child savers were beginning to draw a line in the sand between scientific placement and loose positioning. A godsend to early social workers was the establishment of the Russell Sage Foundation.

Railroad magnate and Wall Street financier Russell Sage died in 1906, leaving his widow a vast fortune, estimated from $60-$80 million. Margaret O. Sage (1828-1918) knew hardship, having been a teacher and spending time caring for her elderly mother. She married Sage later in life. She was intensely interested in social issues. She created the foundation with a $10 million grant for the improvement of social conditions through research, study and publication. (109)

In November, 1907, the foundation's board hired Hastings H. Hart "to make a study of child saving work, carry on propaganda for juvenile courts, or some kindred work." (110) A study was immediately undertaken to ascertain the number of child placements, the methodology used, and which methods produced the best results for children. Thirteen hundred fifty children's homes, child-helping societies and orphan asylums filled out questionnaires. Agents visited organizations and, when allowed, interviewed children in foster/adoptive homes, in eight states: Massachusetts, Pennsylvania, Ohio, Indiana, Kentucky, California, Maryland and Minnesota. (111) Suggested forms for child-placing records were publicized.

In 1917, the State of Minnesota passed the first state legislation mandating investigations of prospective adoptive homes before placement.

The Russell Sage Foundation published a placement manual for social workers, called *Child-Placing in Families* by William Slingerland. (112) Social workers began moving toward factual record keeping and the skilled placement of children.

Ellen Herman, professor of history at the University of Oregon, successfully documented social workers' march toward professionalism in her book, *Kinship by Design*. (113) Children who were placed by compassionate, knowledgeable social workers reaped the rewards of the early-day child savers, who believed all children deserved the best possible outcome.

While Minnesota legislators were convinced early of the need for a social history and review of every triad member (adoptee, birth parents and adoptive parents) before placement, most legislatures resisted change for years. Many states allowed black-and-gray-market adoptions to coexist with agency adoptions, until trafficking in children laws were passed in the 1950s. Independent attorney-facilitated adoptions that fail to utilize social work techniques in determining the best placement for each child are still the norm in some states. Hurley published an editorial, entitled "Selection of Homes," which said it best:

> Many applications are seen at once to be undesirable. Some applicants want a child for base purposes, for beggary or prostitution, or for use in improper exhibitions. Some applicants want children to be passed off upon a husband or other people as their own...Many good people desire children from mixed motives, partly selfish, partly benevolent. They want a child who can be helpful or can furnish company or who will adorn their home by its beauty or intelligence, yet they have a sincere purpose to benefit a child...It is the work of the Society to sift out all applications received, discriminating between those which are inspired by a spirit of love for little children, and those which are inspired by selfish love of the applicants themselves. This discrimination is accomplished partly by the study of the application, partly by correspondence with reliable acquaintances, but chiefly by the judicious inquiry of a trained visitor (social worker), who will often discover essential facts, which do not appear on the initial application or in the letter. (114)

Hurley and the early-day Chicago child savers were aided in their quest to help children by the development of state adoption laws, which is the subject of our next chapter.

CHAPTER 7

ADOPTION'S LEGAL BASIS

During the last 200 years, state legislators spent countless hours developing, debating and reshaping statutes for children, creating new families for orphans, dependent and/or neglected kids and infertile couples. Within the resulting framework, state law recognizes adoption as a contract between birth parents and adoptive parents. A judge divests the birth parents of responsibility and a new couple assumes their place.

However, the very first laws were passed when parents requested to adopt their own children.

Private Laws

Birth fathers requested state legislators introduce private bills that would change the name of their illegitimate children. Those born to unmarried parents take the name of the birth mother. These fathers wanted their children to have their surname. Adoption was gradually added to the language.

The first name change by the Tennessee legislature occurred in1801, when the names of Fanny Lucas and Robert Chapman were changed to Fanny Sappington and Robert Searcy—so they would be on equal footing with the birth fathers' other children, who were legitimate. (115) During the 1803 session of the legislature, one birth father requested altering the names of his eight illegitimate children! (116)

In 1805, state legislators authorized county court judges to make name changes, without asking the state legislature for approval.

> Whereas, the frequent applications to this General Assembly, have become troublesome, and have a tendency to expose the morals of society…Be it enacted…that county courts shall have full power and authority to alter the name of any illegitimate person on application of any person wishing to make legitimate any of their offspring not born in wedlock: Provided, said applicant intends to make said illegitimate person heir, or joint heir, to his estate. (117)

This bill became law on October 3, 1805. On the same day, the legislature approved a second bill, allowing birth father John Henderson to "adopt" his illegitimate son. The son's name was changed from William Miller to William Henderson and the father "hereby adopted the son of the said John Henderson." (118)

The legislature authorized county courts to approve adoptions, beginning in 1852.

> ….the county or circuit courts shall have the power to

authorize and empower any person or persons to adopt any child or children as their own upon application by petition or motion, and the adoption and the names of the parties, and the terms of the adoption shall be entered upon the records of the court, and the court shall have discretion to refuse the prayer of the petition... (119)

Kentucky, Ohio and Minnesota legislatures approved similar private laws, when birth fathers requested their children be legitimized. Kentucky added the term "adoption" to the private laws in 1841, when Willis Roberts adopted his daughter, Louise Warder, as his heir. (120)

Deeds of Adoption

In 1849, Texas legislators passed their first adoption statute. A bill, titled "An Act to prescribe the mode of Adoption," Section One of Chapter XXXIX, read

any person wishing to adopt another as his or her legal heir, may do so by filing in the office of the clerk of the county court in which county he or she may reside, a statement in writing, by him or her signed and duly authenticated or acknowledged, as deeds are required to be, which statement shall recite in substance, that he or she adopts the person named therein as his or her legal heir, and the same shall be admitted to record in said office. (121)

No other requirement was necessary to legally adopt a child in Texas.

A *New York Times* article exposed one of the problems with "deeds of adoption." An adoptive mother from Hardin County, Texas, moved to Tampa, Florida, with her three-month-old baby. She immediately re-recorded the *warranty deed* that transferred ownership of the boy from the birth mother to the adoptive mother.

Florida officials said they believed the deed was illegal, because it deprived the baby of the heritage he would receive with an adoption decree. *The Times* reported, "If the adoptive mother dies before the boy is of age, he would pass as a chattel and become part of the estate." (122)

The early adoption laws of Pennsylvania, Iowa, and Louisiana also allowed parents to adopt children by deed.

Indenture or Adoption?

Some early city ordinances mandated how community leaders were to care for indigent children. Emelyn Peck, a Children's Bureau official, wrote that officials in some cities were required to indenture or bind out poor children until the age of majority. The only prerequisite was that the "destitute minors were liable to become public charges." (123) No parental consent for indenture was necessary. In fact, it could be done over the parent's objections. The indentured child worked for his or her board and room. Girls acted as house servants, cleaning and baby-sitting. Boys were indentured for their ability to perform manual labor. Peck wrote

Many acts relating to destitute children provide for indenture or adoption. (124) In the latter part of the last century, when the movement to take children out of almshouses was in full swing, a tendency away from the harsh indenture laws was also evident. Objection is often raised to child placing, even when it has been carefully guarded by original investigation and subsequent oversight, because of the popular prejudice aroused long ago by the "little slaveys" of the old indenture system. (125)

First Comprehensive Adoption Laws

Massachusetts passed the first comprehensive adoption law in 1851. The legislation provided that any inhabitant of the Commonwealth of Massachusetts could petition a probate judge "for leave to adopt a child not his or her own by birth." (126) Written consent of the child's biological parents, legal guardian, next-of-kin, or "next friend," had to be obtained. Other states, such as Ohio and Nebraska, followed shortly thereafter with their own comprehensive adoption laws.

Illinois' legislators, who deemed it advisable for county judges to decide whether an adoption would be 'in the interest of the child,' passed their law on April 22, 1867. (127) The statute did not require consent from a relative or 'next friend,' if the child was an orphan.

Six years later, in 1873, New York passed its first comprehensive adoption law. If the biological parents were living, they must consent to the adoption. However, if a child had been abandoned, the parent forfeited all rights to the child. A judge could sign an adoption decree without consent six months after the abandonment occurred. (128)

Minnesota Requires Home Studies, Closes Adoption Records

In 1917, Minnesota revised its adoption law, becoming the first state to require home studies of prospective adoptive parents. (129) Lawmakers also closed all adoption files and records to *public* inspection, except for 'parties of interest,' their attorneys, and representatives of the State Board of Control. Other individuals could seek a court order, which would allow inspection of a specific adoption file. (130)

Oklahoma's Adoption Laws

Before Oklahoma was opened to white settlers, tribal law governed all adoptions. The first adoption law for settlers and their children was Nebraska's law. Congress passed the state's Organic Act in 1890, which made all Oklahomans subject to the same laws as Nebraska. County courts handled adoptions. The Organic Act read, "County courts and justices of the peace shall have and exercise the jurisdiction which is authorized by said laws of Nebraska." (131)

In 1893, Oklahoma's territorial legislature incorporated adoption into its own law. The high points of the law included the following: Prospective adoptive parents must be ten years older than the child. A legitimate child cannot be adopted without the consent of the parents; an illegitimate child must have the consent of the mother. Parents who are incapable of giving consent are those who have been deprived of their civil rights: (1) those guilty of adultery or cruelty; (2) those who had been divorced; (3) alcoholics; or (4) those who had been legally deprived of their custody rights, because of abandonment or cruelty.

All parties must appear before the probate judge in the county where the adoptive parents reside. It is the judge's responsibility to examine all the evidence and determine whether the adoption is in the interest of the child. No recommendation from next-of-kin or "next friend" was required.

When the law was modified in 1895, a guardian, or next-of-kin, could give consent if the child had been abandoned, or if the parents were deceased. If there was no next-of-kin in the territory, or the child was a foundling, then the judge was required to determine whether the facts in the case were true, and if the prospective adoptive parents could furnish a suitable home for the child. If so, the judge was to approve the petition for adoption.

While it was thought the adopted child would inherit from the adoptive parents, he was absolutely prohibited from inheriting through "collateral kindred." (132) The adoptive parents and their heirs were not to inherit any property belonging to the child received from his kindred by blood. This act was made retroactive to all adoptions made previously in the territory. The biological parents were relieved of any legal right or monetary responsibility toward the child.

In 1905, Oklahoma's territorial legislature defined the term "Children's Aid Society" as a society organized for the protection of children from cruelty and to care for neglected and dependent children. Section four stated

> Title to child. Any children's aid society to the care of which any child may be committed under the provisions of this Act, shall, subject to the provisions of Section six of this Act, be the legal guardian of such child and all the powers and rights of parents in respect to that child, shall vest in the said society, and it shall be the duty of the said children's aid society to use special diligence in providing homes for such children, legal adoption in such families as

may be approved by the said society, or a written contract providing for their education… (133)

Any incorporated children's aid society could apply to the county commissioners of the county from which a child in their care came, to receive up to $50 for temporary care, in exchange for finding a home for the child and any subsequent supervision that was needed. After paying $50 to the children's aid society, "the county (is exempt) from all further responsibility and expense of said child until it is of legal age." (134)

After attaining statehood, Oklahoma's first legislature imposed the duty of inspecting all maternity hospitals, lying-in hospitals, rescue homes and foundling institutions upon the commissioner of Charities and Corrections. He was to issue certificates, authorizing each facility to operate for one year. He could revoke a certificate after showing cause. He was to issue one-year certificates to all children's aid, home-finding societies, and all institutions "formed for the purpose of adopting into families such foundlings, orphans and dependent children as come into their hands." (135)

In addition, the commissioner of Charities and Corrections shall

> have the power, and it shall be his or her duty to appear as 'next friend' for all minor orphans, dependents and delinquents who are inmates of any public institutions maintained and operated by the State, county, city, or municipality, before any court having probate jurisdiction, and can ask that legal guardians be appointed when it appears that such minor children have an interest in someone's estate, legacy, or property. (136)

In 1910, legislators voted to allow charitable organizations to name the specific guardians for orphan children under their care. When the Whitaker State Home for White Children placed a child into a suitable family home, a written contract was required. The home was to employ a "state agent," to look for indenture homes, and to check on the children who were in homes under the terms of an indenture contract.

Five years later, in 1915, legislators made it illegal for any biological parent to visit and entice a child away (or cause a child to become 'dissatisfied') from any private home where he or she had been placed by the state home. (137) If convicted, they could be fined up to $250. It was a beginning in the march toward sealed records.

Let's flash back to the opening of Oklahoma Territory and focus on the issues of the late 1800s and the early twentieth century with regard to the care of children and adoption issues.

**Figure 1. Lewis Henry Morgan–Photo
courtesy of the Library of Congress.**

**Figure 2. Lester Frank Ward-Photo
courtesy of Special Collections, Gelman
Library, George Washington University,
Washington D.C.**

Figure 3. Alice C. Fletcher-Photo courtesy of
The Peabody Museum of Archaeology and
Ethnology, Harvard, [Peabody ID # 88-56-
10/84070].

**Figure 4. Daniel Boone-Photo courtesy of
the Library of Congress.**

**Figure 5. Sam Houston—Photo courtesy of
the Library of Congress.**

Figure 6. From left, Osage Chief Fred Lookout and Bishop Eugene J. McGuinness at his adoption ceremony. *Southwest Courier*, **January 4, 1958. Photo courtesy of the Archdiocese of Oklahoma City, Oklahoma.**

Figure 7. John Wesley Powell–Photo
courtesy of the Library of Congress.

Figure 8. Orphan Train Riders—Photo courtesy kansasmemory.org, Kansas State Historical Society, copy and reuse restrictions apply.

Figure 9. Rev. Martin Van Arsdale—Photo
courtesy of The Children's Home and Aid
Society of Illinois.

Figure 10. E. W. Scripps, 1912–Photo courtesy of the E. W. Scripps Collection, Mahn Center for Archives and Special Collections, Ohio University Library.

Figure 11. Painting of the Oklahoma Land Run of 1889−Photo courtesy of Barney Hillerman Collection, Oklahoma Historical Society Research Division, photo by Meyers Photo Shop.

Figure 12. E. W. Marland–Photo courtesy of the Oklahoma Historical Society Photograph Collection, Oklahoma Historical Society Research Division.

Figure 13. Lydie Marland–Photo courtesy of the Ponca City News Collection, Oklahoma Historical Society Research Division.

Figure 14. Charles N. Haskell–Photo courtesy Frederick S. Barde Collection, Oklahoma Historical Society Research Division.

Figure 15. William H. Murray–Photo
courtesy of Frederick S. Barde Collection,
Oklahoma Historical Society Research
Division.

**Figure 16. Kate Bernard–Photo courtesy of
the Oklahoma Historical Society
Photograph Collection, Oklahoma
Historical Society Research Division.**

Figure 17. Mabel Bassett–Photo courtesy of
the Oklahoma Historical Society
Photograph Collection, Oklahoma
Historical Society Research Division.

Figure 18. Pearl Holmes and Anna
Witteman—Photo reprinted from *Mother
Lee's Experience in 15 Years' Rescue Work*
(Omaha, Nebraska: privately printed, 1906),
p. 226.

Figure 19. Oklahoma Rescue Home, Guthrie
Oklahoma—Photo reprinted from *Mother
Lee's Experience in 15 Years' Rescue Work*
(Omaha, Nebraska: privately printed, 1906)
p. 219.

Figure 20. Home of Redeeming Love,
Guthrie, Oklahoma—Photo reprinted from
*Mother Lee's Experience in 15 Years' Rescue
Work* (Omaha, Nebraska: privately printed,
1906), p. 230.

Figure 21. Home of Redeeming Love in
Oklahoma City—Photo courtesy of the
Barney Hillerman Collection, Oklahoma
Historical Society Research Division, photo
by Meyers Photo Shop.

Figure 22. Reverend J. D. Schollenberger–
Photo reprinted from *Mother Lee's*
Experience in 15 Years' Rescue Work
(Omaha, Nebraska: privately printed, 1906),
p. 222.

Figure 23. Creekmore Wallace—Photo
courtesy of the Oklahoma State Archives.

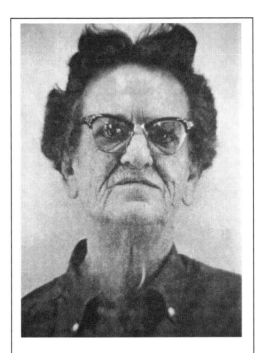

Figure 24. Mae Marshall—Photo courtesy
Oklahoma County Sherriff's Office.

Figure 25. Mae Marshall's Private Home for
Unfortunate Girls—Photo by the author.

Figure 26. Mae Marshall's Private Home for
Unfortunate Girls, rear view–Photo by the
author.

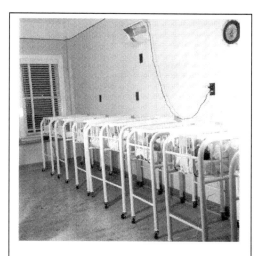

Figure 27. Edmond Hospital Nursery,
1947–Photo courtesy Edmond Historical
Society Photographic Collection and the Hal
Doolittle Collection.

**Figure 28. Current picture of the old
Edmond Hospital—Photo by the author.**

PART B: STATE ISSUES

CHAPTER 8

OKLAHOMA PIONEERS

Thousands of pioneers heeded Horace Greeley's call to "Go West." Many of them stood at the starting line of Oklahoma's Land Run, waiting to hear the gunshot that would signal the beginning of a new life in their 'adopted' state.

April 22, 1889. 11:59:50. Riders hunched atop snorting horses. Mules pawed the earth. Muscled arms and chapped hands tightly gripped the reins of animals hitched to covered wagons. Women clutched children, huddled on wagon beds.

Anticipation rose with every breath of air.

Soldiers raised their pistols toward the sky. Bang! Bang! Bang! Shots pierced the spring day.

Men and animals lunged forward, gulping clouds of red dust. Hundreds of pioneers pounded into Oklahoma to stake their claims.

The offer of free land drew men, women and families from near and far to the starting line. They brought with them everything to survive: grain, farming tools, linens, sourdough starter, foodstuffs, cooking utensils and clothing. Each brought his professional implements. Some brought children. Others would send for their families after they were settled. All individuals brought with them their unique cultural heritage.

This heritage, received from their parents and other elders in the original communities of their youth, gave the new Oklahoma Territory citizens some basic ideas of how to solve the problems of child care in a land where disease, lawlessness and death would be common.

But no one thought of that on the day of the Land Run. The priority was being the first to stake their claim. A few pioneers were shot early-on, when disputes over land claims erupted.

United States soldiers were the only law in the territory. Within the first two weeks, towns elected city officials so violence could be curtailed through ordinances.

Orphans appeared from the beginning, when violence or disease cut short the lives of even the youngest parents. Illegitimacy and infanticide also occurred and the new Oklahoma Territory citizens looked to the customs of their former homes to solve current problems.

All original (white) state government leaders left their native states to "adopt" Oklahoma as their new home. Some were men called "squaw Indians," who married Indian women and settled in Oklahoma before the run. Others established their residence on or soon after April 22, 1889. These larger-than-life characters were men and women who had a tremendous inner drive to make their own way in the world and establish a state that would be more to their liking than the one they left.

Adoption was on the minds of the early-day Oklahomans, as

evidenced by printed handkerchiefs and flyers, urging the joining of Oklahoma and Indian Territories into one state. The following advertisement was circulated around Chickasha, Oklahoma.

> Mr. and Mrs. Will B. State
>
> Announce
>
> The marriage of their adopted daughter
>
> Indian T.
>
> To
>
> Mr. O. K. LaHoma
>
> March 6, 1906
>
> at Washington, D. C. (138)

Oklahoma became a state on November 16, 1907. The people celebrated the occasion by staging a marriage between Oklahoma and Indian Territories in Guthrie, the capital city.

Like any marriage, there were good and bad times. Pressures within and without the state commanded the attention of officials and molded public opinion.

The Republicans were considered the party of big business. Oklahomans usually sent Democrats to the state legislature, hoping to be protected from what they saw as big trusts pushing down the quality of life for the working class.

Democrats from that era were conservative, too. However, there were other obvious differences in the men and women who formed the Democratic caucus in the legislature. Some legislators always voted for issues that were favorable to the rural areas.

Others always supported urban issues. Some supported the cattle and beef industry. Others were more interested in good roads. Every legislator wanted to have a junior college in his own backyard. The economic pressures of the new state, plus the agitation of special interest groups, created tension-filled meetings and definite opinions about the care and fate of children within its borders.

Many early-day Oklahoma leaders were orphans, or half-orphans, and had good reasons for supporting adoption. Here are the stories of three principal Oklahoma leaders, who helped shape the state's attitude toward children:

William H. Murray–president of Oklahoma's Constitutional Convention

William H. Murray, "Alfalfa Bill," grabbed a front line position in Oklahoma politics when he was elected president of the Constitutional Convention in Guthrie on November 21, 1906.

Murray's political base came from his newspaper, *The Blue Valley Farmer*, which he published in Tishomingo, Oklahoma, and distributed to state farmers. Through the paper, he became familiar with all the agricultural issues and met many of the small business entrepreneurs.

Murray's grandparents were the first settlers of Grayson County, Texas—just beyond the Oklahoma border to the west.

His mother died in childbirth when he was 15 months old. Murray and his older brothers ran away from home when he was twelve. They stayed with a tenant farmer and his wife. Murray said Grandma Lopez was the only mother he ever knew. When she died, Murray wrote "the mother of babyhood may be found renewed in the breast of another." (139)

His first job was teaching school, while he studied law at night. After passing the bar (it was an oral exam and he says they didn't ask him any questions), he practiced law in Fort Worth and then moved to Tishomingo, the capital of the Chickasaw Nation. He became familiar with the Indian culture and their method of caring for orphan children.

Murray married Alice Mary Hearell, niece of Douglas H. Johnston, governor of the Choctaw Nation. After the marriage, Murray paid $50 for a 'citizen head-right' to become a member of the tribe. (140) It allowed him to practice law in Indian court. He represented many Indian children whose white guardians were stealing their land. (141)

When Murray was elected to head the Constitutional Convention, he used the opportunity to write a new state constitution based on his own populist views. He wanted to limit big business and allow farmers and small businesses to flourish without a lot of state regulation.

Legislators were also restricted from passing any law that would affect the estates of minors. No legislature could authorize the adoption or legitimation of children. (142) Those bans are still in effect. (143) Judges were to appoint guardians for children. Adoption was not specifically mentioned as a duty of the court.

In order to get enough Congressional votes for the passage of the new constitution, Murray needed the support of labor. Labor leaders wanted to have a position called the commissioner of Charities and Corrections. The office would protect workers and their families by inspecting all institutions and advocating for children. The idea was criticized from one end of the country to the other, including harsh words from President Theodore Roosevelt. But Kate Barnard, and other supporters of children and labor, wrote hundreds of letters to the president and Congress, asking them to accept the new constitution. It worked. Murray's radical constitution was approved.

Charles N. Haskell—Oklahoma's first governor

Haskell had two mothers. His father died of pneumonia in Leipsic, Ohio, when the boy was three. His birth mother was left with five children to support. In the 1860s, widows usually "bound out" their children to someone, or several individuals, for support and education. Mrs. Haskell refused to do that.

Instead, she worked as a janitor in the Methodist Church for $5 per month. She also worked late every night as a seamstress to keep her family together. (144) The children earned money by doing odd jobs for neighbors.

Lydia McConnell Miller and her husband watched the young Haskell grow. She taught his Sunday school class. In 1870, their six-week-old son died. Mrs. Miller asked Mrs. Haskell if they could take 11-year-old Charles home with them to take their son's place.

"We are so lonely without him. We want to take your Charles home with us to take the place of our Charles." (145)

Mrs. Haskell could not refuse to ease Mrs. Miller's pain. She allowed Charles to live with the young couple, but she did not release him for adoption.

You must let him return, if that is what he wants to do, she told her.

So Haskell moved from his mother's home in Leipsic, Ohio, to a farm outside of town. During the day, he cleared land, built fences and helped market the farm's produce. He gave his earnings to his mother in town. At night, his foster mother taught him all the common school subjects. He studied so hard that he passed the exam to teach school at age 17. Most school board members believed a 17-year-old was too young to be a teacher. William Krause, a friend of Haskell's deceased father, offered him a position with the Medarie School. Haskell promised Krause that he would work as hard at teaching school as his father had worked at being a cooper (barrel-maker).

After his students had gone home for the day, Haskell studied law. He was admitted to the Ohio bar. In 1881, he resigned his teaching position and opened a law practice in Ottawa, Ohio. Many clients sought his services and he won a good percentage of those cases. Business fired his imagination and he built several railroad lines in Ohio. He was invited to visit Muskogee, Oklahoma. He liked the town so well that he moved there to build railroads in and around Indian Territory.

When he was elected to the Constitutional Convention from Muskogee, Haskell served with distinction as the floor leader. He would have been elected vice-president under Murray, but he placed Pete Hanraty's name in circulation for that position to bolster the support of labor. Haskell was then prepared to run for governor. After serving as Oklahoma's first governor, he retired from public life and returned to his Muskogee law practice.

His birth mother and his foster mother were equally proud of his accomplishments.

Kate Barnard—Oklahoma's first Commissioner of Charities and Corrections

Kate Barnard has been described as "Oklahoma's Joan of Arc." (146) She was the first woman to write part of a state constitution. She was the first elected female state official. She was also the first woman to create a state department. This was all before women were allowed to vote.

Rachel Shiell Mason was a widow with two boys when she married J. P. Barnard in 1873. Kate was born on May 23, 1874, in Thayer County, Nebraska.

When Kate was only three, her mother died following childbirth. The baby died, too. Barnard sent her step-brothers to be raised by their maternal grandparents. He kept Kate with him as he roamed the grasslands of Kansas surveying and lawyering.

As the Oklahoma lands were being opened for settlement, Barnard put Kate in a Kansas convent, so he could make the run on his own. She spent three years with the Catholic sisters, while her father tried to build a life in Oklahoma. He lost his first claim but he managed to hang on to a second. He bought a small home in Oklahoma City and sent for her. She was appalled at the poverty of neighborhood families who did not have warm clothing and often went hungry. Kate finished high school and passed the exam to teach school. She moved to her father's claim near what is now Newalla, Oklahoma, in eastern Oklahoma County. She taught school for a short period of time. The extreme poverty and the absence of students who had to work in the fields left a vivid impression on the young woman.

Kate went to business school and was appointed stenographer to the Democratic Party in the territorial legislature. While working in Guthrie, she wheedled an appointment as secretary to a group going to the St. Louis World's Fair, where Oklahoma would have a booth. She met Roy Stafford, a reporter on the St. Louis *Post-Dispatch*. She and Stafford toured the slum areas of St. Louis.

When Kate returned to Oklahoma City, a new relief organization couldn't pay its bills. The merchants, who had organized the Provident Association, appointed Kate to be its director. She moved the headquarters into her home, which saved the rent money. Next, she contacted Stafford, who had become an editor for *The Daily Oklahoman*. Stafford ran an appeal for food and clothing for the association in the newspaper. Items poured in. The donated clothing quickly filled the house on Reno Street, where Kate lived with her father. (147)

Kate marshaled volunteers to sort and deliver clothes to the needy.

In 1906 Stafford sent Kate to St. Louis, Chicago and Denver to meet with charity workers in those cities. She mailed columns back to the newspaper. She met with Jane Addams, founder of Chicago's Hull House, and others to formulate the best laws for children and labor in Oklahoma.

While she was away, there were three large families, who were particularly needy. It took most of their funds to help them. This angered many people in and out of the association. They said she was too young to run such a big relief effort and they didn't like it that she had received her salary while she was in St. Louis. Kate resigned on April 22, 1907, to run for the office of commissioner of Charities and Corrections.

Some of her fellow reformers chided her for jumping into politics. She responded

While most of the leaders in the charity movement deplore the fact that politics should enter our field, I cannot agree with them. I believe that if our people would get out and help elect friends of our measures and defeat our enemies, we should accomplish a great deal more than we can do by getting women's clubs, churches, etc., to pass resolutions and look wise. (148)

She stumped the state for the opportunity to put into place the mechanisms that would make the lives of children and families better. And she won.

Imagine her shock when she looked for her office in the capitol building. She found it in a corner of the third floor, hiding behind a sign for the men's toilet. Furious, Kate wrote

I had battled up from the bottom…poor, motherless, lonely…often desperate…I had achieved my laurels by the hardest, dirtiest, most thankless job in civilization (caring for the sick and hungry poor)…my whole life had been one long, lonely Gethsemane…I expected Happiness when I reached the State House …This is what I got…a hole in the wall…in the attick…hidden away under the projecting roof of an alcove…behind the foul odors and flaming placard, "Men's Toilet." I shall never forgive Haskell and Murray for this attempt to befoul my Soul. Let them answer if they can… (149)

Perhaps her fury at the insult only served to fire her ambition to protect the rights of Oklahoma citizens. She marshaled through a juvenile court bill. In 1909, she pushed through a child labor bill that released hundreds of children from work in laundries, mines and factories. She shepherded through a new compulsory education law, where children from ages eight to sixteen would be required to attend school. (150) She inspected all jails, hospitals and children's institutions in the state.

If any coordinated state welfare effort was needed, the task fell to Charities and Corrections. Kate answered individual queries for help by referring them to the voluntary agencies, such as the Provident Association, the Home of Redeeming Love, or the Oklahoma Children's Home-Finding Society. Depending on the circumstances, she sometimes called on individual churches for help. Investigations of the Cornish Orphans Home and the Nazarene Rescue Home were carried out during Kate's tenure.

She rallied national experts to write articles on social issues and children for *The Daily Oklahoman.*

Her biggest battle was for the rights of Indian orphans. Guardians were stealing royalties and land from the children. She appointed an attorney, Dr. J. H. Stolper, to act as "next friend"—to go to court for the orphans to stop the abuse of the guardians' power. Fifty-eight of those children were in the state's Whitaker Orphan Home. (151) Three children were found living in the woods, unwashed and uncared for. Others were held prisoner until they turned 18, when they were induced to sign over their land to the guardian. (152)

A small group of legislators tried to wreck her department over this issue. They appointed an investigating committee to consider charges against Stolper. Committee members found their hands were tied and their power was limited. The legislature voted to cut funding for the department in hopes Barnard would drop her crusade for Indian children. It didn't work.

A committee of county judges met to formulate rules for courts to follow when adjudicating guardianships for Indian children.

(153) Every guardian would be required to make an annual report to the court. All receipts and assets must be accounted for. A final accounting could not be made unless the minor appeared in court. Justices were beginning to take an interest in protecting the rights of children.

Kate chose not to seek re-election in 1913. She traveled to Denver, Colorado to regain her health while under the protection of Denver Juvenile Court Judge Ben B. Lindsey. She was 56 when she died—a sick and embittered old maid in a downtown Oklahoma City hotel in 1930.

Barnard's legacy was the creation of the legal mechanisms that gave children a small degree of protection from the elements. Unfortunately, there were thousands of other circumstances in children's lives that were not under the control of the commissioner, or the officials who followed in her foot-steps. Our next chapter begins to chronicle some of those situations.

CHAPTER 9

DUMPSTER BABIES

"Dumpster babies" aren't a new phenomenon in the twenty-first century. Even in early-day Oklahoma, orphan—or abandoned—babies were trashed.

When the nude body of a baby boy was found in an old shoebox under some shrubbery outside the Delmar Gardens Theater, Oklahoma City police called it child murder.

"Many times bodies of infants have been found about the city, in old wells, under walks, hidden in shrubbery and weeds," a police spokesperson said. (154)

Infanticide touched all parts of the state—rural, as well as urban. The media publicized some cases.

On May 26, 1887, the *Vinita Indian Chieftain* reported the conviction of Mrs. Sarah Fields, a Delaware Indian, for the crime of infanticide of her illegitimate grandchild. (155) She received the death penalty. Her daughter, the baby's mother, was also charged, but the jury dead-locked eleven jurors to one for her conviction. She was to be re-tried at a later date. No follow-up articles were published.

The *El Reno News* reported a woman arrested in October, 1896 and charged with killing her newborn infant. (156) The body of the infant had been found six months earlier in Cottonwood. No details of the trial could be found.

In southern Oklahoma, the bloody body of a baby was found lying on top of a farmer's woodpile. Upon investigation, the deputy sheriff found bloodstains on the bedding of the farmer's son and his new wife. They had been married 10 days. A physician examined the young woman and found she had just given birth. The couple was arrested. (157) When the husband's case went to trial, the charge against him was dropped for lack of evidence. (158) No record of the mother's case could be found.

In Elk City, Oklahoma, another newborn died at the hands of her mother. A landlady discovered one of her renters clutching a newborn baby's throat, as she hysterically beat its tiny body against the hard wood floor. The baby died a short time later.

"I would give a thousand dollars never to have seen that child," she is quoted as saying. (159)

Authorities asked the mother about the father of the baby. She said she was married to a Mr. Anderson in Elk City, but no record of the marriage could be found. (160)

The jury acquitted the mother. An editorial about the verdict said the whole community was in sympathy with the mother, because "many a young girl is led astray by a scheming villain (the baby's father)…" (161)

Other babies of unmarried parents were sent to 'baby farms,' where they died, or were warehoused, until adoptive parents could be found.

Baby Farms

The term baby farmer was brought into popular usage in the mid-1800s in England. They were women who advertised their service of boarding babies. Many of these 'boarder babies' died, because the women could not handle the number of infants in their care. Infant births were not required to be registered in England until 1874. During a six-month period in 1759, 2,271 foundlings under one-year-old were found on the streets of London. (162) In 1870, London police reported finding 176 exposed bodies of babies. (163)

Mary Boyle O'Reilly publicized problems with the management of baby farms in the United States in two issues of the *New England Magazine* in 1910.

As a trustee of the Children's Institutions of Boston, O'Reilly became concerned about advertisements in Boston newspapers from baby farmers in Nashua, New Hampshire, just across the state line.

She posed as a prospective adoptive parent to gain information about the business. In order not to jeopardize the investigation, O'Reilly didn't use real names or addresses. She called one home 'The House of Forgotten Children.' Upon inquiring about a ten-day-old baby girl, who was advertised for adoption, she was told the baby had died of a 'wasting sickness.'

In the second installment, O'Reilly investigated the 'House of

Unwanted Babies.' The nurse of the 'Unrecorded Infants' admitted giving laudanum to the infants to make them sleep. When she was asked if any of the infants had died, the woman replied in the affirmative. "One Monday and one today. But they were weak little things," she said. (164)

Upon inspection of the farm, O'Reilly believed the babies were neglected. She reported the undertaker said "farmers always call late at night." One farmer advertised that actual confinement for the birth mother would cost $30. Adoption cost $50 more. If all charges were paid up front, no record would be made and "....absolute disposal..." was guaranteed—whatever that meant! (165) Over half of the infants in the 'House by the River' became unclaimed babies in Woodlawn Cemetery. They were buried by public charity in the Stranger's Lot. O'Reilly concluded

If 65 percent of all such miserable mites will die in some House by the River within the month of their surrender, it grows obvious that little children faced less cruel danger in the days of Herod, the King. (166)

Baby Farms—Oklahoma City

A number of birth mothers in Oklahoma City placed their babies directly with a *baby farmer*, agreeing to pay the woman $2-$3 per week, plus $10 at the time of the adoption. (167) Other birth mothers gave their babies to the Oklahoma City police matron. She would place the infant with a baby farmer, who would look for prospective adoptive parents.

Lizzie Clark was one such baby farmer. Although she couldn't sign her name to the warranty deed of her property, by 1908 she had placed 150 babies in adoptive homes from her business in baby trafficking. In the 1910 Oklahoma census records, Clark is listed as the wife of John Clark, 717 East Chickasaw (now Fourth Street), and the mother of four children. The husband's occupation is listed as wagon-driver.

After the body of a baby was found in a pine grocery box near the railroad tracks on West Third Street in Oklahoma City, Justice William H. Zwick held an inquest to investigate the "promiscuous distribution of babies about the city on doorsteps, baby farms, railroad tracks and river banks." (168)

Clark and an Oklahoma City physician were subpoenaed to testify in the investigation. (169) It was reported that the doctor delivered some of Clark's babies at Bethany Hospital, and then paid her to keep them until adoptive homes could be found. (170) No charges were filed. Clark said she stopped accepting babies from the Bethany doctor, because he would not pay her increased charges. (171)

In spite of physician-assisted births, some babies were not lucky enough to survive being jostled from one home to another. Three-month-old Ruth Fuchs died in a foster home after being bounced from birth mother to Police Matron Nora B. Hill to Lizzie Clark and then to foster parents. (172)

Another little one, deserted by her mother and left with foster parents at 18 months of age, couldn't find a permanent home. Police Matron Hill refused to take her. County Physician Clutter said he wasn't running an orphanage. "If we find the mother, we'll send them both to the poor farm." (173)

Two months later, the police matron placed a six-month-old baby boy with a prospective adoptive couple, who refused to give their names.

They absolutely refused to give their names, but gave me
sufficient references by which I determined their ability
and circumstances…these people will adopt him as soon
as the papers can be drawn up. (174)

The birth mother also refused to give her name.

On February 14, 1908, Mrs. Nettie A. Bond became Oklahoma
City's new police matron. Within one week, she announced the
Provident Association would take care of all babies, whose parents
were unable to care for them.

"The Provident Association will have direct control of the
charity work." (175) That promise didn't last long.

Two months later, she personally gave an abandoned baby girl
to Mrs. Frank Robbins. Robbins said she thought she could adopt
the infant. (176) Bond decided the baby was being neglected, so
she transferred the baby to the care of Mrs. Clare Battin. Since Mr.
and Mrs. Battin were moving from Oklahoma City, she agreed to
allow Mr. and Mrs. John W. Hall to adopt the baby. While the
Halls were petitioning Judge Sam Hooker to adopt the baby,
Robbins kidnapped the child from Battin's home. The baby spent
several days with Robbins, but Judge Hooker forced the woman to
give the baby to Children's Aid. (177) Mrs. Battin took over the
care of the child, while permanent plans could be made. The baby
was then four months old. Mrs. Bond refused to comment. (178)

Oklahoma babies, who were fortunate enough not to be placed
with baby farmers, were parceled out to one of several orphanages
that were established by churches or voluntary associations for
their care until a foster family or an adoptive home could be found.

Some children received good care, while the care of others left
a lot to be desired. Public policy and state law were still in the

formative stages.

Oklahomans were always suspicious of state-run relief programs. To a large extent, individuals insisted on doing their own charity work. This made the whole system very disorganized. (179)

"Disposition of Orphans" was the name of a thesis submitted to the University of Oklahoma in 1911 by Bachelor of Arts' candidate Mary Grace Lee. She highlights two systems used to deal with orphans: the institutional system and the home-finding system. Critical of the large barracks used in some asylums, Lee advocated the cottage-type environment, where some "mothering" could occur.

In her remarks about home-finding, she said it was "almost universally conceded now that a good family home is far better for a homeless, dependent child than any institution." (180)

But she found that system flawed, too.

"The greatest evil in the home-finding system arises out of the habit of some institutions of placing-out children on any terms or no terms at all, and then abandoning them," she wrote. (181) She did not define "placing-out." It is not known whether she meant foster care, indenture, adoption, or all three.

Here is a description of several of the more publicized orphanages in early-day Oklahoma.

Whitaker Home for White Children

W. T. Whitaker, an Indian merchant in Pryor Creek, Indian Territory, became concerned about the territory's white children, who had no parents. The Indian tribes and their governments took care of the dependent Indian children, but there was no one to look after the white children who had been abandoned, or whose parents were deceased or incapacitated.

Whitaker and his wife began by taking in a few white orphans in 1881, but the numbers of children escalated and the home became an orphanage.

In 1904, the Cherokee orphanage at Salina, Kansas, burned. Whitaker offered to take the children. He spent so much of his own money on the children that he became personally broke. (182) He lobbied Congress for aid. In 1907, he gave the institution to the state. The legislature named it the Whitaker Orphan Home of the State of Oklahoma. (183)

State agents were supposed to oversee the home and protect the welfare of the children. In December, 1915, Victor (Jill) was convicted of the statutory rape of (Susan Jones), an 18-year-old former resident of Whitaker. The *State Sentinel* of Stigler, Oklahoma, reported the story of Jill's trial:

(Jill) was charged with going to Pryor, Oklahoma, the state orphan's home, where the girl was enrolled and selecting her, as he told the superintendent that he wanted a girl to play with his own daughter...

(Susan Jones) was the first witness for the state. She told how (Jill) had taken her out of the home at Pryor. She stated that when he got to the door of the home that he selected her at a glance, among the many other girls present. She says she was in a classroom in the fourth grade. (184)

(Jill) received a seven-year sentence to be served in a

maximum security prison at McAlester, Oklahoma. Commissioner of Charities and Corrections William D. Matthews requested a copy of the indenture contract by which (Jill) was permitted to take the victim from the home. (185) No other information is available.

When Whitaker overflowed its capacity in 1917, the Oklahoma State Legislature authorized the building of another state orphanage to serve the western half of Oklahoma. The Western Oklahoma Home for White Children was located in Helena, Oklahoma. A state agent made arrangements to place-out children from this institution.

Oklahoma Children's Home Society

Brought to Oklahoma City by real estate developer Anton H. Classen and his wife, the Oklahoma Children's Home Society was chartered May 4, 1900. Sometimes called the Children's Home-Finding Society, its purpose was to find placements for homeless children.

Eva Wells, M.D., a graduate of Epworth University School of Medicine, served as the attending physician for the society at 1539 West 24th Street in Oklahoma City. (186)

In an undated issue of the society's newsletter, "Oklahoma Children's Home Finder," on file at the Oklahoma State Historical Society, the editor lists the society's purposes: (1) to investigate reports of child neglect or abuse; (2) seek homes for children and investigate the character of the applicants; and (3) place and visit the children in their foster homes, and take them back, if necessary, and continue supervision until they are adopted or turn eighteen, the usual age of majority.

The society received all illegitimate babies born at the Holmes'

Home of Redeeming Love for placement into adoptive or foster homes.

Two of Oklahoma's commissioners of Charities and Corrections, Kate Barnard (1907–1915) and Mabel Bassett (1923–1947) referred prospective adoptive parents to the society. Letters to that effect are on file at the Oklahoma State Archives.

Commissioner Bassett responded to an inquiry from a Frederick, Oklahoma, physician about placing an illegitimate baby with the society. She wrote

> You understand that the baby must have a complete physical examination and be free from any taint of congenital loss or other history that is likely to cause it to be defective in any way. I have been trying very hard to stop the adoption of defective children and hope that every physician in the state will cooperate with me in carrying out this very important plan. (187)

Superintendent N. B. Dunham wrote Commissioner Bassett that they had cared for 400 children in 1924. Thirty went back to their parents and 328 were placed in permanent homes. The letter does not specify that these children were adopted. According to documents at the Oklahoma Historical Society, the society closed its doors in 1929 for lack of funds.

Agency records were turned over to Commissioner Bassett. A newspaper article in *Harlow's Weekly* said she ordered a thorough investigation of the society. Of the 4,000 case records given to the commissioner, 600 children, or 15 percent, could not be found. After an intensive ten month study by a member of Bassett's staff, 545 of the 600 children were located, which meant that 55 children were never found. (188) The Oklahoma State Archives are currently holding all of these case records. A court order is necessary to access them.

Cornish Children's Home (1903)

Moses and Ellen (Hackler) Harris were young teachers in the Chickasaw Nation in southern Oklahoma in 1903. There were no public schools. All schools in the territory were subscription schools, which required tuition. Many poor children and orphans could not afford to learn to read and write. Harris wanted to brighten their future, so he rented a building in Cornish for homeless children. Later, he moved the children to 297 acres near Cornish, Indian Territory. He named the agency the Cornish Children's Home. The children who lived at the home

....have been taken from poverty-stricken, insanitary and sometimes lawless environments and placed in the home-like, Christian atmosphere of the Cornish Home. Here they stay as welcome members of the big family until they are voluntarily adopted by some approved couple. (189)

In 1911, the Oklahoma State Legislature appropriated $5,000 for the care of orphans in this private institution. (190)

On October 2, 1911, Wynnewood, Oklahoma's, *New Era* newspaper published an article about five children from Garvin County who had been placed in the Cornish Home. The story began, "Superintendent M. E. Harris of the Cornish Orphans Home was in Wynnewood Saturday, looking after the interests of his home here..." (191) Harris expected the counties to help subsidize the home when they committed children to his care.

An unsigned copy of a letter, dated January 24, 1913, from Oklahoma's commissioner of Charities and Corrections Kate Barnard to Harris was found at the Oklahoma State Archives. The letter detailed the results of an investigation into allegations of cruelty at the home, which were made in affidavits signed by Harris' neighbors. Barnard interviewed each child separately. She found some children had been placed in gunnysacks, which were tied up on ladders, so that, if they moved around very much, the ladder would fall down. Sometimes buckets of cold water were thrown on them while they were in the sacks.

The commissioner also alleged "that children had been placed out carelessly and without the necessary adoption papers or inspection or supervision of homes..." (192)

Barnard wrote Harris,

Because complaints have been heard and evidence rendered that children were carelessly placed in unsuitable homes, I hereby order that hereafter you will take all children before the juvenile courts, and have a careful record made of their transfer, so there'll be no difficulty in locating them should it become necessary or desirable; and further, that all contracts for placing out of larger children, be filed for my inspection. (193)

According to the commissioner's directive, Harris fired the matron. He saved the home by asking the commissioner to help him make good and correct the problems in his institution. The commissioner replied, "We have all made mistakes...I am especially anxious to co-operate with you to the end that this institution will become one of the best in the state." (194)

Two children were removed from the orphan's home as a result of the abuse. Citizens' groups were formed in several towns to monitor improvements at the home. Women's groups in towns like Marlow, Oklahoma, made quilts and other clothing for the children.

Treatment of the children may have improved, because Lillie Floyd has fond memories of living there after 1929. She has kept a list of most of the children who were committed there. Diane McCornack, the librarian in Ringling, Oklahoma, has a copy of Ms. Floyd's list. (195)

Sand Springs Orphans Home (1908)

Charles Page was never elected to public office, but he touched more lives at a deeper level than most famous politicians.

His humanitarian odyssey began on a cold, bleak day in Wisconsin in 1871, when his weeping, widowed mother stood over a steaming washtub. Her tears mixed with the hot soapy water.

Don't cry, Mother, eleven-year-old Charles told her. When I get big, I'll take care of you. And I'll help other widows and orphans, too.

He never forgot his promise—or his vision. He saw himself building a town from the ground up.

Beginning as a telegraph dispatcher in his teens, he worked his way into business and eventually came to Oklahoma to cash in on the oil boom. With his earnings, Page helped many people in Tulsa. Through Salvation Army Captain B. F. Breeding, Page gave food and shelter to hundreds of people who were down on their luck. He also gave a monthly pledge to an orphanage called Cross and Anchor, which was located north of Tulsa.

As part of his growing business interests, he bought 160 acres of Indian land northwest of Tulsa. It had clear, spring water and lots of trees. This is where he decided to build his town.

In 1908, Breeding resigned his commission with the Salvation Army to manage the property for Page. When desperate or sick people came to Page, he sent them to the farm for Breeding and his family to look after. He gave them jobs to help clear the land.

Business associates told Page the Cross and Anchor Orphanage was facing bankruptcy, so he took off work to investigate the rumor at its source—the orphanage itself and its superintendent.

The first children he saw were six siblings—five girls and a boy. They crowded around him. He picked up the three-year-old, but she wriggled off his lap and hid behind her ten-year-old sister.

She just got back from being adopted, one sister told him. She wouldn't stop crying and they brought her back. She thinks you might want to take her away, too. Page was horrified.

Author Opal Clark recounted Page's subsequent conversation with the superintendent in her biography of Page, entitled *A Fool's Enterprise*.

"I want to know by whose authority you have been tearing families apart?" Mr. Page asked. "All those poor little kids have is each other. The home is not set up as an adoption center. It was supposed to help children, not tear their hearts out."

"We had to do it," came the response. "There's not enough money coming in to feed them. We've borrowed and mortgaged everything just trying to keep food on the table. We thought we should try to find homes for those we could. The place is due to go into receivership right away and I don't know what we will do with the rest of these children. Older ones are harder to place."

Mr. Page wrote out a check and handed it to the man. "Try to hold the creditors off as long as you can. This should feed the children until I can figure out something." His voice was always lower when he was emotionally disturbed. He tried to keep the tears out of his voice.

"These poor little helpless kids...Don't tear anymore families apart through adoption. I'll see that they are fed and what to do about the debts."

As he turned to go he said once more, "No more adoptions unless it's an only child. Do you understand?" The man nodded and thanked him for the check. (196)

After knocking on many doors in Tulsa to no avail, Page asked Breeding if he could send the children to the farm. The former Salvation Army captain and his wife agreed to take the children, with Page's assurance that he would provide all the monetary necessities.

More and more children were sent to the farm as Page heard about families who needed help. Eventually, a large children's home was built on the property. Page and his wife Lucille would eat Sunday supper with them.

He loved it when the children all ran out to meet him. Some Home children had parents, but for one reason or another, they couldn't take care of them. One mother asked Page to take her three little girls, because she had nowhere for them to go while she worked. Page believed the children were too small to be left alone all day, so he accepted them. When the woman re-married, she came to reclaim the girls. Two weeks later, she brought them back, saying the marriage didn't work out. They were accepted again. In another three weeks, she returned with another man, wanting to take the children again.

Page was angry. Clark reports this is what happened when he talked to the mother.

"Children are human beings with feelings and emotions," (Page told the mother). "They are not boomerangs to be thrown out and grabbed back. They need stability and security. If you take them this time, you can't bring them back. It's up to you. Which is it going to be?" The woman left the girls in the Home. Mr. Page knew he was going to have to do something to protect the children from being snatched back and forth from relatives, and never having a feeling of permanency and belonging, never being able to adjust to either situation. He began legal proceedings that would give him full custody of the children. This way, he would be the one to make decisions as to their welfare. Rules were made that a parent could take a child from the Home once, but she could never bring the child back. (197)

As Page's oil business flourished, he worried about what would happen to "his kids," when he was gone. He formed a corporation to administer the Sand Springs Home and allied industries. He named the original board members. But in his will, he chose the grand master of masonry to appoint the successors, following his death. He was not a mason himself, but he had been impressed with the caliber of some of their members. He felt the grand master would appoint people who were as diligent as he was in performing the duties to keep his home open in perpetuity.

Page died suddenly of pneumonia in 1926.

Orphanages formed by Religious Organizations

St. Joseph's Catholic Church in downtown Oklahoma City supported an orphanage from its earliest days. The Methodist Church operated a children's home in Britton, and the Baptist Children's Home was also on the north side of Oklahoma City. The Church of Christ supported two orphans' homes in the state, one in Tipton and the other in Frederick, Oklahoma.

Most of the children placed in these homes were not free for adoption, because parents were unwilling to sign the relinquishment forms. The children were not considered abandoned, because arrangements had been made for their care.

The next chapter details religious organizations that supported pregnant women and helped them plan for the adoption of their unborn children.

CHAPTER 10

RESCUE HOMES

Rescue homes appeared in the late 1800s as shelter for pregnant women who had no place to go. Families arranged for their daughters to enter these facilities to hide their pregnancies from neighbors and others in the community. Usually staffed by zealous Christians, the mission of these early maternity homes was to convert birth mothers and provide homes for their children by adoption.

Deaconess Hospital's Home of Redeeming Love

The Home of Redeeming Love is the oldest and most enduring maternity home in Oklahoma. It is a voluntary, non-profit organization and a mission of the Free Methodist Church. Founded in Guthrie, Oklahoma Territory, as the Oklahoma Rescue Home, it has evolved into a 250-bed metropolitan hospital in Oklahoma City. Its name was changed to Deaconess Hospital with adoption services provided through a department called Family Services.

Their workers have processed over 20,000 cases to the present.

The home was originally a spin-off from Omaha's Tinley Rescue Home and the Wichita Rescue Home, which were both supported by individual Free Methodist churches.

Rev. J. D. Schollenberger suggested a rescue mission in Oklahoma because so many Oklahoma women were entering the Wichita home. (198) On December 30, 1900, Omaha evangelists Lydia A. Newberry and May P. Dougherty held an organizational meeting at Guthrie's Presbyterian Church and a board for the new rescue home was quickly formed. (199) Also involved in the initial organization were Mrs. Della Jenkins, wife of the secretary of Oklahoma Territory, along with Mrs. Pearl Holmes and Mrs. Annie H. Tannehill. (200) The women lobbied church members, business leaders and territorial representatives for donations. Three months later, they moved into a house, located at 1021 East Noble Avenue, within one mile of the capitol building of Oklahoma Territory. (201)

On January 11, 1902, the *Oklahoma State Capitol* newspaper published the home's annual report. Twenty-six women had been in the home during 1901. Ten of the 26 were still being cared for. Six babies had been born during the year. (202)

Anna Witteman transferred from the Wichita home to Guthrie to free Mrs. Newberry and Mrs. Dougherty to move northwest to establish a rescue home at Enid, Oklahoma. Witteman's tenure as superintendent spanned almost 50 years. A member of her family has served as administrator for the balance of its history.

The following story is a reconstructed scene, depicting Witteman's entrance into Oklahoma.

*   *   *

Wichita's Tremont Street teemed with carriage traffic and pedestrians.

A young woman and a bearded, middle-aged man stood on the porch of a three-story brick building. Each floor had a balcony, framed with wooden latticework and resembling houses in the French quarter of New Orleans. "RESCUE HOME" was printed on a banner hanging from the third floor. The couple stepped down, hurrying toward a covered wagon, parked at the street's edge.

Two adolescent boys lounging across the street hooted and pointed toward the young woman.

Anna ignored them. She was used to their laughter and stares. She had worked at the Wichita Rescue Home for a year. (203) At 28, she looked the same age as many of the inmates of the home. It was a demanding job. And now she was off for a new adventure— Oklahoma Territory!

Anna looked up at the high seat in the front of the wagon. Grasping a handle at shoulder level, she gathered her dark muslin skirt around her legs, stepped on a wheel spoke, and pulled herself up.

"Miss Witteman, let me help you," Rev. Schollenberger said.

Anna looked down at his rotund form.

"Thank you, sir. But I am quite capable. Remember, I rode in a wagon much like this one from Warren County, Ohio, to Wichita as a child," she answered.

Deflated, the reverend turned his head toward the baggage being loaded into the back.

"It won't be long now, Miss Witteman. The trip to Guthrie will be much shorter."

Sitting down, she placed their bread and butter sandwiches on the floor next to her feet.

Schollenberger's round face turned red as he hoisted himself up into the seat beside her.

"You'll like Guthrie, my dear. I promise. There won't be so many people critical of your age. They have been begging for a matron. Mrs. Newberry is both superintendent and matron. They won't care whether you're 28 or 128, as long as the job is done," he told her.

Crack! The reverend snapped the reins. The wagon lurched forward. Anna grabbed the wooden seat to keep from falling.

When they reached the edge of town, Schollenberger turned the wagon south, toward the Kansas state line.

He handed Anna the reins. "Here, my dear, you can control this rig just like everything else in your life."

She took the reins, but ignored his comment.

"You will find a fertile field for your talents in Guthrie," Schollenberger said. "Girls there need a woman of your character to help them see the error of their ways."

Anna blinked. "My mother would be happy with my work. Mama thought women in the brothels were terrible. How could they just abandon their babies? She was horrified when she read George Eliot's novel, *Adam Bede*. (204) How could a woman kill her baby?"

Schollenberger rolled his eyes toward the sky. "That question is as old as time. Oklahoma newspapers published an article about an infanticide in Oklahoma City on the very day we had our first meeting to organize the rescue home. (205) If you can teach them to be mothers and to leave their old way of life, that's well and good. If not, they must give up their right to be mothers."

The horses kicked up a cloud of dirt. Anna coughed.

"It would be heart breaking to lose one's baby," she told him.

"If they cared about the baby, they would turn their life over to God. But ninety-nine percent of these women can't wait to get back to the brothel. That's why adoption is so important. A God-fearing family can take the child and raise it—not knowing anything about its awful parentage," he said.

"We were all adopted by God when we were born again. Being twice adopted would be that much better!" she exclaimed. (206)

"Precisely, my dear," Schollenberger replied. "The Free Methodist Church's district superintendent sent me a book called *Delia, the Bluebird of Mulberry Street.* (207) Have you heard of it?"

"Yes, Reverend Schollenberger, would that I could save a soul such as Delia! Emma Whittemore was a saint. I am not worthy to walk in her shoes, but God has called me to the rescue field," she told him.

Anna remembered the wrath of her parents when members of their church board gave money to a single woman with two babies. Her father's face had contorted and he bellowed that they would lose their minister if they couldn't pay his small salary. "That money belonged to the church and not to any grass widows. (208)

They don't deserve help!"

Her mother countered, "At least the babies are innocent!"

"Yeah," he shot back. "They'll grow up to be just like her!"

Anna vowed at that moment to go into rescue work. And her dream of working in the mission field on a new frontier was close at hand—The Oklahoma Rescue Home.

*   *   *

As soon as Witteman became familiar with The Oklahoma Rescue Home, Newberry and Dougherty moved to Enid, Oklahoma, where they established another home, specifically for girls coming from jails and brothels. Newberry wrote,

> In almost 20 years of rescue work (in our four homes), we have proven there are two distinct classes of erring girls. One, young girls ruined in their trust in man's promise of marriage, who know nothing of a life of debauchery and sin. Another class of girls from the jails, saloons and brothels is steeped in sin. To mix these two classes would be a menace to the least erring and out of the divine order—God has so arranged it that the Enid Home of Redeeming Love holds out a Savior's arms of love and mercy to those the Guthrie home cannot admit. (209)

Brother John Colson donated the land for the Enid mission, while Mrs. Pearl Holmes donated land on South Perkins for a new building in Guthrie. To honor their benefactress, rescue workers changed its name from the Oklahoma Rescue Home to the

Holmes' Home of Redeeming Love. (210) Sometimes it was called the Holmes' Hospital.

Funding was always a problem at the home. While the national Free Methodist Church supported foreign missions and services to Native American Indians, individual churches selected home missions and supported them on their own, without any funding from other churches. Some chose to support local rescue missions.

On March 23, 1909, the Home of Redeeming Love at Guthrie and at Enid proposed to merge and relocate in Oklahoma City, if residents could provide a five-acre building site and $10,000. (211) The directors believed having only one location would help their financial situation. Governor Charles N. Haskell and commissioner of Charities and Corrections Kate Barnard immediately applauded the suggestion. (212)

The Guthrie property was sold to Dr. John W. Duke, M.D., Oklahoma's first commissioner of Health.

The directors of the maternity home secured a parcel of land at 5401 North Portland in northwest Oklahoma City for the construction of a two-story red brick building to house the girls and the labor and delivery rooms. The officers of the rescue home were: president, Lydia A. Newberry; vice-president, Anna H. Tannehill; treasurer, Pearl Holmes; superintendent, Anna Witteman; matron, May P. Dougherty; and financial agent, M. Simpson Allen.

Walter W. Wells, M.D., was named head of the medical staff. Babies relinquished for adoption were placed through the Oklahoma Children's Home-Finding Society. Dr. Wells' wife, Eva, served as the medical director for the society.

A plea for donations to the home appeared in the March 31,

1911 edition of *The Daily Oklahoman* to help finish construction.

Judge Dickerson from Chickasha, Oklahoma and an unnamed fellow called "Pilgrim Stranger" heaped praise upon the maternity home. The article said most of the girls were motherless. They came from one hundred fourteen different Oklahoma towns. Of five hundred girls, seventy-three came from Oklahoma City; fifty from Guthrie; thirty-five from Enid; thirty each from Muskogee and Shawnee; fifteen from Chandler; fourteen each from Lawton and Ardmore; twelve from Kingfisher; seven from Anadarko; six from Ada; and other towns from one to five. The balance came from other states.

The erring girl was described as the "most vicious, lazy, lustful, depraved, unruly victim of the underworld...soul and body rest at the Home brought each one back to health, virtue and God." (213)

Pilgrim Stranger, who was probably M. Simpson Allen, repeated the views of the social purity movement. He wrote that the segregated districts of prostitution, with unsanitary tenements, disorderly houses, and vile snakes who traffic in women are a social evil that promote the fall of girls from even the best homes. (214)

A farm surrounding the institution provided food for the patients and staff. William and Florence Butterfield, Anna Witteman's brother-in-law and sister, moved to Oklahoma City in 1917 to manage the farm. Their son, Ralph Edson Butterfield, a fifteen-year-old teenager, came with them. Later in life, he became a minister in the Free Methodist Church and an administrator of the hospital.

Over the years, a number of the rescue workers in the home

became deaconesses in the church. Some of the women taught at the home's small nursing academy.

In 1924, Gladys Irene Henderson graduated from the nursing school. She married Ralph Butterfield in 1926. A year later he graduated from Oklahoma City University. His first employment was teaching elementary school in the Putnam City Public Schools near the maternity home. Gladys's sister, Phyllis, married Martin Andrews, who became a northwest Oklahoma City physician, and Witteman's personal physician.

When the Oklahoma Children's Home-Finding Society closed its doors in 1929, the home began functioning as an adoption agency.

Twin boys, available for adoption, were born at the home in 1933. On April 10 of that year, *The Daily Oklahoman* ran their picture on page one in hopes of finding adoptive parents for the babies. Rescue workers wanted the children to be adopted together. (215) The paper did not follow the story to tell readers if an adoptive couple was found.

By 1935, thirty-five hundred babies had received care at the home and many had been placed for adoption. (216) The average number of women at the home was seventy-four. Two hundred forty-six girls and their babies were cared for in 1937. (217)

Lee M. Jones, the employee assistance representative for Southwestern Bell Telephone Company, who was responsible for the support and counseling of many female telephone operators, was named president of the hospital's board of directors.

Money was always scarce at the home. During the1930s, the deaconesses opened a small hospital to the general public to help defray expenses.

County commissioners from Jackson County (Altus, Oklahoma) signed a contract with the home's board to pay a monthly retainer fee so the home would be available to any unwed mother from that county. The Oklahoma Attorney General's Office nixed that idea. The written opinion said it was against state law to pay for care that was not designated for a specific patient.

In 1942, Bishop Charles V. Fairbairn reported in *The Free Methodist* that the Home of Redeeming Love would be allowed by the church's board of administrators to request donations from any church in Oklahoma or Texas. (218) These two states would be called the home's "patronizing area," in which they could solicit funds and secure special offerings.

The Oklahoma City Hospitality Club and other volunteer groups donated equipment and funds to keep the maternity home afloat.

In addition to Deaconess Hospital's Home of Redeeming Love, four other well-known maternity homes operated in the Oklahoma City area for much shorter periods of time.

Amie Rescue Home

Mrs. Nettie Bond, a pre-statehood Oklahoma City police matron, established the Amie Rescue Home at 201 N.E. 10. She hired Miss Abbie Matthews to serve as matron.

On August 8, 1905, an article appeared in *The Daily Oklahoman* that alluded to rumors of mismanagement at the home. The board of directors of the home resigned, and the work was turned over to the city's women's clubs. (219) There was no investigation.

Before the town's rumor mill subsided, Judge Harper subpoenaed Mrs. Bond to testify in a court case about the character of a thirteen-year-old girl. Bond defied the court by having her physician send a note to the judge, which said she was too ill to appear in court. (220)

Three days later, Bond charged into the home with a revolver and threatened the women.

"It was intimated that Mrs. Bond, using her authority as police matron as a club, was endeavoring to scatter the patients and break up the institution," the newspaper reported. (221) It also said she wanted them to vacate the premises by two p.m. the following day, even though some of the girls did not have shoes or adequate clothing.

When police arrived, Bond was arrested for disturbing the peace.

Her hearing was scheduled for the next Saturday evening with Judge Hayson presiding. During five hours of testimony in front of a packed courtroom, Matthews and all of the girls in the home testified against Bond. The prosecution argued that she was an intruder in the home. Bond's defense was that the building had been her home, her belongings were still there, and she was responsible for the girls until other arrangements could be made for them. Judge Hayson acquitted Mrs. Bond. (222) The home closed.

Oklahoma City Maternity Hospital

When the open door at the Amie Rescue Home slammed shut, Mayor Henry Scales realized there was no non-sectarian home in the city to send pregnant girls for care. He initiated the remodeling of the old city waterworks plant at 530 West Elm (now S.W. 12th street) as a rescue home with seven beds. Private donations furnished the home. The Oklahoma City Maternity Hospital opened in April, 1909. Mrs. Lulu Brashear worked as resident matron. Dr. J. W. Riley, city commissioner of health, visited the home daily. (223) It closed in the 1920s.

Nazarene Rescue Home

In 1905, Mattie Mallory-Morgan and Reverend J. B. McBride organized a small rescue home to exist cooperatively with the Oklahoma Orphanage in the Beulah Heights Addition of Oklahoma City. (224)

On October 26, 1906, an interdenominational school, sponsored by the Oklahoma Holiness Association, was also established at that location. For three years, the orphanage, rescue home and college operated under the same management.

An early-day female evangelist wrote that "….churches, orphanages, rescue homes and schools sprang up to prepare workers for the harvest field…(they) trained students to be pastors, evangelists, missionaries and teachers." (225)

In 1908, representatives of the Oklahoma Holiness Association and other small Holiness groups from all parts of the United States met at Pilot Point, Texas, to form the Church of the Nazarene. Rev. C. B. Jernigan was appointed superintendent of the Oklahoma-Kansas District.

Then, in 1909, the Beulah Heights School was transferred to a board of trustees, appointed by the Oklahoma Holiness Association. When the association turned the school over to the

Nazarene Church, a new site was chosen for the school in what became Bethany, Oklahoma. The college is now known as Southern Nazarene University.

Mallory-Morgan traded the rescue home's property for land adjacent to the new campus. Mrs. Johnnie Jernigan, wife of Rev. C. B. Jernigan, became superintendent of the rescue home at the new location.

During Mrs. Jernigan's tenure, writes Leona McConnell, buildings were erected and property values increased to $15,000.

For seven years, Mrs. Jernigan gave herself untiringly to the care of wayward girls in this Home. Seven hundred girls registered there during her superintendence. Many of these young women were converted while in the Home, and restored to lives of respectability and usefulness. (226)

On April 16, 1913, assistant commissioner of Charities and Corrections Herbert M. Peck held a hearing to determine the management policies of the Nazarene Rescue Home.

A transcript of the hearing is on file at the Oklahoma State Archives. The complaint that precipitated the investigation is missing. The documents indicate a Mrs. Welch filed the complaint. She was a former matron who did not get along with Mrs. Jernigan, the superintendent.

The first witness was Reverend W. H. Roberts, who lived three miles north of the home and conducted religious services for the girls. He had four brothers who were in rescue work at Pilot Point, Texas. He testified that Mrs. Jernigan received no salary, but was allowed to keep forty percent of the donations that were earmarked for the rescue home.

Charges and counter-charges flew during the hearing, but this discussion will be limited to how adoption was administered at the home.

The following is the verbatim testimony of Mrs. Jernigan, in regard to adoption procedures in the home:

PECK: "What charge then do you regularly make for placing the baby?"

JERNIGAN: "$25, if they can pay."

PECK: "And if they can't? You will take what they can pay?"

JERNIGAN: "Yes."

PECK: "What does that go for?"

JERNIGAN: "For the expenses of running the home."

PECK: "It is not spent for the purpose of adopting the baby?"

JERNIGAN: "I do not adopt them. I simply place them."

PECK: "They sign a paper releasing their claim on the child?"

JERNIGAN: "Yes."

PECK: "What paper do they sign—have you a copy of the paper?"

JERNIGAN: "I can get one."

PECK: "Then these girls, after they have given birth to these babies, sign a paper practically abandoning their babies?"

JERNIGAN: "If you want to call it that. I do not call it that."

PECK: "To whom do they release their baby, to you or to this home, or another one?"

JERNIGAN: "I placed two babies, one in the Davenport home and one at Enid. They are the only ones I have placed."

PECK: "How many babies has the home placed in the last year?"

JERNIGAN: "I do not know how many in the last year, but I believe only 25 since the home has been running."

PECK: "Do you advise the girls that come here to give birth to have their babies adopted?"

JERNIGAN: "I leave that to the girls. I tell them that is for them to settle and if they want to adopt their babies out they can do so." (227)

Peck called Mrs. Madero, a former matron, to testify. She alleged that Mrs. Jernigan did indeed tell the girls they should adopt out their babies.

When Mrs. Jernigan was recalled as a witness, Peck continued his questioning:

PECK: "What record do you keep of the disposition of the babies that are adopted on?"

JERNIGAN: "Keep it on here." (Indicating) (228)

PECK: "Have you got on there a record of where each baby is placed?"

JERNIGAN: "Yes, sir."

PECK: "For instance, that girl (that just) left here—among the items of expense she paid was $25.00 for having her baby placed. Where is that baby?"

JERNIGAN: "It is with Mrs. D. in Jackson County."

PECK: "Who paid the expense of taking that baby down there?"

JERNIGAN: "They came after it."

PECK: "Has that baby been legally adopted?"

JERNIGAN: "I do not know."

PECK: "You do not follow that up?"

JERNIGAN: "No, sir." (229)

George Matlack, attorney for the home, asked Mrs. Jernigan why she didn't follow up on the status of the babies. She replied that she had "too much to lose in time and expense." (230)

After a few more questions about notary fees for signing the relinquishment forms, the witness was dismissed. The last line of the transcript read, "Investigation closed." (231)

The home remained open.

Mrs. Jernigan retired in 1916, due to health problems. The District Assembly voted to close the rescue home. The property was transferred to the college.

Our Lady of Victory Maternity Home

Unmarried mothers began finding their way to the office of Father James A. Garvey, superintendent of Catholic Charities, in 1927. For two years, the women were sheltered in private homes. Our Lady of Victory Maternity Home and Nursery, 811 Northeast Eighth Street, Oklahoma City, opened in 1929. The babies were allowed to stay in the nursery until adoption or age three, when they were transferred to St. Joseph's Orphanage. In a 1940 column in the *Southwest Courier,* Father Garvey wrote

> Our Lady of Victory Maternity Home and Nursery is gleaning the souls of many infants from the same broad highway that leads to eternal ruin. We have never had so many girls with babes in arms walk in from the streets to sign their children over to us for adoption into good Catholic homes. (232)

During the 1970s, the home was moved to a larger facility in Bethany, Oklahoma. An order of nuns, called the Felician Sisters, staffed the maternity home.

Another order, called the Sisters of Mercy, worked in the church and school in Father Garvey's parish, Holy Angels.

The Sisters of Mercy was an order founded in England by Mother Catherine McAuley, an adoptee.

When McCauley was fourteen years old, her mother died. Her father decided she would be better off with another family. Her chosen adoptive parents were well-to-do English people who were thrilled to have her. After they passed away, she opened their home and used her inheritance to establish the Sisters of Mercy in England. The new order spread to the United States and the first Sisters of Mercy came to Oklahoma in 1884 to teach in the school connected with Our Lady of Victory Catholic Church in Purcell, Oklahoma, twenty miles north of Pauls Valley.

Hundreds of babies were adopted through Catholic Charities, headquartered at Holy Angels Church with Father Garvey, and later, with Father Isenbart. Both priests wrote many editorials for the *Southwest Courier*, the weekly Catholic newspaper, praising the work of the rescue home and the ability of the church to place babies in good adoptive homes.

Our next chapter outlines the media's role in the early history of adoption.

CHAPTER 11

EARLY-DAY MEDIA

Before computers and the internet, before television and talk shows, the information highway in America consisted of newspapers and national magazines.

Here are some examples of how the media handled adoption and children's issues.

SAN FRANCISCO—Hearst Newspapers

Newspaper magnate William Randolph Hearst began his newspaper reign in San Francisco on March 3, 1887, with a series of three stories in the *Daily Examiner* about the deaths of illegitimate babies. (233)

"Olga Eugena" was a two-day-old baby girl who died on February 28, 1887, after being abandoned at the basement door of a foundling asylum. A hospital attendant saw the wagon-driver deposit the baby, but he could not identify him.

Birth mothers, or others, frequently placed babies in baskets that were attached to the buildings of several foundling hospitals within San Francisco. The ringing of a bell was to notify hospital personnel that there was a baby in the basket needing care.

Nurses loved to feed and cuddle the healthy infants who were left at their door.

Other times, they cried over the bodies of dead babies, poisoned by massive doses of drugs to still their crying for the trek down the city's streets to the basket. Mothers, who were frightened of being "found out" with a babe in their arms, would miscalculate the amount of drugs necessary to quiet the little one. The baby would be given so much narcotic that he or she would never wake up, even with the ministrations of the hospital personnel. Babies also died when individuals did not ring the bell. They died from exposure to the elements, freezing temperatures, rain and snow, with little or no covering on their tiny bodies.

The reference to adoption in this series of articles occurred in the last paragraph of the third story. A matron of one of the foundling asylums is quoted as saying:

In broad day, upon one occasion, a child was placed upon the steps, naked and unwashed. It was a dreadful sight, and yet it lived and thrived and has a good home now across the bay. (234)

OKLAHOMA CITY—E. W. Scripps' *Oklahoma News*

Newspaper editors increased their readership by printing the sad stories of babies, whose parents were unmarried and unable to care for them. The articles tugged at readers' hearts with throbbing questions: Would the orphaned child have a home? Would the childless couple find a baby to love? Which couple would be chosen to be the baby's parents? Would the story have a happy ending?

Building suspense in stories day-after-day, the penny press newspapers promoted adoption by focusing on the empty arms of the adoptive parents and the orphan's sad state of affairs.

Oklahoma City's penny press was called *The Oklahoma News*. As part of the Scripps-McRae Press Association, publication began October 1, 1906. Editors believed they could market a newspaper to the working class for a penny because the other papers cost a nickel and contained long articles about political situations.

E. W. Scripps (1857?–1926), the power behind the chain, believed laborers, housewives and common people wanted short news items and human interest stories that would touch their hearts.

The chain began during the 1800s with four newspapers: *Detroit Evening News, Cleveland Penny Press, Cincinnati Post*, and the *St. Louis Chronicle*. (235) Bent on expansion, Scripps plunged into the medium-sized markets, avoiding the larger cities like Chicago and New York City, where competition was too intense. By the time the Oklahoma City paper was established, the chain held papers in towns from Ohio to the west coast, including Terre Haute, Evansville, Memphis, Nashville, Dallas, Denver, Pueblo, Seattle, Sacramento, San Francisco, Los Angeles, San Diego, and others. Every editor was responsible for sending breaking news from his geographic area to all of the other papers in the chain.

When Scripps dropped Milton McRae as a partner and added Roy Howard, the name changed to Scripps-Howard.

He also began the News Enterprise Association (NEA), a wire service that sent feature material and human interest news briefs to every paper in the chain. Robert F. Paine (1856-1940), a close associate of Scripps, was named to run NEA and take on the editorial supervision of all the newspapers. Scripps ordered the editors to use NEA features and to make them account for 25 to 35 percent of each issue. This meant that one-third of the news copy was

under the direct control of central management...
editors had little influence inside the chain. Scripps and
a handful of senior managers were the de facto editors
of much of the content of the chain's newspapers. (236)

Scripps controlled the kind of news reported in his papers. As editorial head of the chain, he and Paine advised editors on what was interesting to readers and how to grab readers' attention with photographs and sketches.

In addition to managing a newspaper empire and building a ranch in LaJolla, California, Scripps loved to read. One of his favorite authors was Charles Dickens, whose tales such as *David Copperfield*, *Oliver Twist*, and *Great Expectations* centered on the fortunes of orphans.

The Canadian-born Dionne quintuplets fascinated Scripps. Their physician, Dr. Allen Roy Dafoe, believed the poor parents could not provide adequate care—including incubators, uncontaminated milk, and clean clothing for the five little girls. The government wrested guardianship from the parents and gave the job to Dr. Dafoe. He built a nursery across the road from the parents' farm home. Dafoe barred the mother and father from visiting the babies for long periods of time. The girls became a side-show attraction, as hundreds of onlookers traveled to see them in their nursery.

Scripps negotiated a contract through the NEA to provide his readers with daily pictures of the girls during their first year of life.

The chain also distributed articles through the Scripps-Howard Newspaper Alliance. One of those articles "Only Parents Illegitimate" was about the California Department of Health removing the words legitimate and illegitimate from birth certificates. The impetus for this decision came from a ruling by California Superior Court Judge Leon R. Yankwich. A case came before him involving two unmarried parents. The father was seeking to wrest custody of the baby from the mother. Judge Yankwich told the courtroom, "There are no illegitimate children, only illegitimate parents." (237)

Scripps was always looking for new markets, where he could expand his readership. In 1925 his eyes focused on a small Albuquerque newspaper with a scrappy lawyer for an editor.

Carl Magee was an Indiana-born lawyer, who established a pre-statehood law practice in Tulsa, Oklahoma. Mrs. Magee's health was poor. Her lungs needed the dry air of New Mexico. When his wife had been in Albuquerque almost a year by herself, Magee closed his law practice, moved to Albuquerque, and purchased the newspaper. He fought government corruption wherever he found it.

Magee was giving his best, but the moneyed interests in New Mexico kept pushing him down. His back was to the wall. He faced bankruptcy. Scripps bought the paper to keep Magee's fight alive. Eventually, the little Albuquerque paper helped bring down the Secretary of the Interior and exposed the Teapot Dome Scandal, which involved pipeline use in Wyoming.

After four tumultuous years in Albuquerque, Magee was grateful when his wife's health permitted a return to Oklahoma. The chain transferred him to *The Oklahoma News* in 1927. Magee had learned his lessons well. He splashed the names and pictures of orphan babies on the front page.

Magee assigned an excellent, young reporter to write a consumer column under the pseudonym of "Mr. Fixit." His task was to hear reader complaints about garbage service, potholes [yes, there were potholes in 1929], or other problems. He tried to answer every question readers brought to his desk. His columns were the result of using his journalistic skill to tell readers about the problem and finding a solution that seemed to be the best for all concerned.

Part of Mr. Fixit's job included finding adoptive parents for orphan babies.

It was like an advertising campaign. The paper printed the picture of the baby on the front page and invited prospective parents to contact him. Judge C. C. Christison, Oklahoma County probate judge, approved ten adoptions that were facilitated in this manner. So many childless couples clamored to be chosen as adoptive parents that Mr. Fixit published a list of orphanages, where couples could apply for a child to adopt. (238)

Here are several cases, publicized by the *Oklahoma News* that shed light on adoptions in the late 1920s and early 1930s.

Story One—1929

As five-month-old "Baby Doe" lay in his crib, Mr. Fixit crafted an emotional appeal for adoptive parents. The first headline said, "A Happy Boy, Ready to Make a Home of Someone's House, Asks Aid of Mr. Fixit." (239) The baby was in the Oklahoma City General Hospital, waiting for new parents. His mother had already signed a relinquishment form. Many couples answered the front page ad for a home for Baby Doe.

Six days later, the newspaper announced County Judge Christison had approved an adoption for the baby. Mr. and Mrs. Walter Billingsley of Wewoka, Oklahoma, were the proud new parents. (240)

Mr. Fixit facilitated nine more uneventful adoptions through the *Oklahoma News* and Judge Christison. When he hung up his "fixit" pen four years later, LeRoy Plumley unmasked himself. He described his experience as Mr. Fixit. He also updated the progress of one of his successes, 'Baby Doe' Billingsley. He said the foster parents, Mr. and Mrs. Billingsley, were still happy to have the little boy. They had been one of the first couples to inquire about the baby. Billingsley even sent a picture of the boy to run with the follow-up article. (241)

Story Two—1930

"Police Seek Mother of Two Months Old Girl Abandoned in City Roominghouse,' was the January 7, 1930 headline for the *Oklahoma News*. (242) Under the baby's picture was printed the child's name, "Maxine---?" No by-line appeared.

Two sisters had left the baby in their room at a hotel, after checking in for the night. One told the clerk they were going to the bus depot to pick up their suitcases. They would be right back.

They never came.

Proprietor Mrs. A. H. Bales turned the baby over to Mrs. Bertha Gist, director of the county social service bureau. When the baby was examined at the Oklahoma General Hospital, a hospital label with the name "Maxine" was found on her back. The last name had been torn off.

Police detectives matched the hospital labels. Maxine's label originated at the Home of Redeeming Love. Rescue workers tapped their records for the baby's mother. She was a 15-year-old unmarried mother from a small oil field town, east of Oklahoma City.

Judge Christison scheduled a hearing and subpoenaed the girl, the baby's father and the grandparents.

"Maybe the mother wants Maxine back…if she will come back for her child, I will talk to her about raising it,' Judge Christison said. (243)

The *News* ran a picture of Judge Christison with Baby Maxine and three nurses on January 10, 1930.

"If it becomes necessary to adopt Maxine out, somebody is going to get a wonderful child," Judge Christison said. (244)

Three days later, the *News* reported Christison had transferred the baby from the hospital to the Home of Redeeming Love until a decision could be reached. They also publicized Christison's criteria for adoptive parents:

1. Citizens of Oklahoma would have preference over out-of-state couples;

2. Residents of Oklahoma County would have preference over other Oklahoma couples; and,

3. A Christian environment would be more important than a wealthy environment.

Christison also said he did not want to give the baby to a society matron who would leave the baby with nursemaids. (245)

When a blizzard dumped inches of snow on the ground the day of the hearing, Christison wasn't surprised no one appeared. He re-scheduled it to make certain the mother had every opportunity to reclaim her child. (246)

On January 23, 1930, the newspaper reported Judge Christison and the Home of Redeeming Love had received a letter from Maxine's mother, pleading for the baby's return. Christison said he had always believed the young mother would come back. He said he believed the older sister coerced the mother into abandoning her baby.

> Her love (the mother) is strongest of all. She would go through life broken-hearted. It would be giving her not only lifelong pain to be deprived of her child, but would mean that Baby Maxine would go through life without knowing her mother. I could not be the one to have Maxine living in one town in the state and her mother in another, both going through life 100 miles apart without seeing, knowing and loving each other. I knew she would write… (247)

The mother asked if the Home would keep the baby until she could make arrangements to take her. On February 1, 1930, Christison gave Mr. And Mrs. Vaughn A. Campbell temporary custody of Maxine—just until the mother could reclaim her. Mrs.

Campbell said they would adopt the baby, if the mother did not appear. (248)

Baby Maxine's last picture and article appeared on March 10, 1930, the day after the mother came for her. They were re-united at the foster parent's home. The mother's name was not printed, at her request.

Mrs. Campbell said she would like to adopt both baby and mother, because the mother was just a child herself. (249)

In a subsequent article, Christison said he believed unmarried mothers made the best mothers, because they knew all about teenagers' pitfalls, and they could help their children avoid them. (250)

Adoptions in Oklahoma County averaged one per day throughout the Great Depression.

"The biggest change…during the Depression," Christison said, "is the number of young couples moving in with their parents and, as a result, giving up their child." (251)

Stories Three and Four–1930 and 1935

Two other adoption stories of note appeared in the *Oklahoma News*. One occurred in 1930, and the other in 1935. There were similarities in the two cases. No names were given. There were no pictures. The women had been married, but divorces were pending. They each had an older child and said they could not afford to feed another baby. Both mothers said they never wanted to see their child at all. (252)

Reporter Noel Houston wrote that the first pregnant mother

"did not dare look at it for a moment. For if she looks into its eyes, she knows she can never bear to part with it." (253)

The Oklahoma News received a flood of phone calls about the unborn babies.

In one column, the reporter said a rich banker and his wife had been chosen to be the adoptive parents of the first baby. "If the wealthy couple get it, the child will always know them as mother or father," Fixit wrote. (254)

In the second case, the pregnant mother said, "I don't want to see the baby. If I did, I never could consent to give it up." (255) Thirty-nine couples applied for her unborn baby. A childless Oklahoma City couple was chosen to be the baby's parents by the birth mother's attorney.

This was the last big adoption case covered by the Oklahoma News. On February 9, 1939, three weeks after introduction of the sealed records bill in the Oklahoma state legislature, it ceased publication.

National Magazines

Editors of national magazines worked day and night to keep abreast of the latest information for their readers. Competition between magazines grew fierce. Conversations about topical stories abounded in barber shops, drug stores and other gathering places across the land. Stories about adoption were among the subjects that prompted lively discussion.

Saturday Evening Post. In 1920, Irvin S. Cobb, a humor/fiction writer for the *Saturday Evening Post*, publicized the plight of orphans when he included in a column about various charities the story of a baby sold to a couple for $2.00.

Mitty, a black laundress, purchased an immigrant family's baby. She became exasperated with the little one and wanted her money back. The family had already spent the $2, and they didn't want the baby back.

"The baby wasn't a real white child anyway, and not worth the two dollars she'd paid for it," Cobb wrote. (256)

Hygeia. In July, 1924, the American Medical Association's journal *Hygeia* published an article about how to "correctly" adopt. Author C. V. Williams, superintendent of the Illinois Children's Home and Aid Society, told readers to use a responsible adoption agency, so that they would receive a child with no probability of physical or mental defects.

Williams suggests defective children be placed in foster homes, paid for by the communities from which they came. Normal children need adoptive homes, he said.

Bring together these lonely children and these childless families, and the blessings to family and child are reciprocal. The child rejoices that he has found a father and a mother; the parents that they have acquired a great blessing and responsibility in the care of a child whose future will depend on the environment they create. (257)

Woman's Home Companion. One of the first national articles on black market adoptions appeared in the December, 1944, issue of *Woman's Home Companion*. The main purpose of the article was to call for state laws that would oversee the decisions made by independent baby brokers.

Author Virginia Reid said Children's Bureau officials estimated over half of the adopted illegitimate babies were placed "by individuals or quack agencies at a substantial profit." (258)

Single individuals or loosely knit groups could easily fly under the radar, facilitating gray or black market adoptions. Some brokers ratcheted up their fees on the backs of adoptive parents. Others didn't always get signed consents or relinquishment forms from the birth mothers. Sometimes adoptive couples received children who were not healthy.

In one case an adoptive couple contracted to adopt twin boys before they were born. The first boy died within a few days after birth from hydrocephalus. The seemingly normal baby was tested, but the results indicated he was afflicted, too.

If they (the adoptive parents) had waited for a few months, put up with the red tape involved in supervised adoptions, the family would have the assurance that the child they adopted was free from disease…There will be 'baby brokers' wherever there are unscrupulous people who put personal profits above human welfare and happiness. But there must, at least, be laws under which these brokers can be brought to account. (259)

Reid's call for tougher laws against baby brokers fell on deaf ears. The U. S. Supreme Court had long ago stepped back from adoption issues by giving to each state the right to regulate all adoptions within its boundaries—no matter how the child came to be within its borders. (260)

Let's explore how the Great Depression and the political issues of the day impacted Oklahoma's adoption policy.

CHAPTER 12

OKLAHOMA IN THE 1930s

As Oklahoma families spiraled downward during the Great Depression, well-meaning citizens looked for answers to the "orphan problem."

County judges and commissioners were responsible for children in the rural areas. Both Oklahoma City and Tulsa had social service agencies that served urban needs. The Children's Joint Case Committee investigated all reports of abused and/or neglected children in Oklahoma City. They provided temporary emergency care, medical treatment and recommendations for adjusting the child's home circumstances, to "relieve the community of the expense of the care of the child." (261) Sometimes their workers recommended adoption. This voluntary agency handled a total of about twelve hundred children's cases during the early 1930s.

E. W. Marland, Oklahoma's ninth governor, had a special interest in adoption, because he was an adoptive father. Here is his personal story.

Marland's personal adoption story

On the north central Oklahoma plains, where Ponca Indians once roamed and the 101 Ranch was built, oil producer E. W. Marland struck black-gold.

An elderly Indian, named "Running After Arrow," heard the gusher roar beneath the earth's surface. He watched in disbelief as the fuel spewed from the soil toward the sky. He told Marland that the sounds and sights were a bad sign.

"Uh-h. No good, no good," Running After Arrow said. (262)

Marland ignored the old Indian. Success in the field would help him control over one-tenth of the world's oil production. What else could a man want? He had a large home in Ponca City, a wife whom he adored, and two adopted children.

His children were Lyde and her natural brother George—the two oldest children of Mrs. Marland's sister and her husband. Their family lived in Flourtown, Pennsylvania. George was born in 1897 and Lyde followed on April 7, 1900. The father was a pushcart peddler. Everything was all right in the birth family for a while, but money became extremely tight when more children were born.

Marland and his wife were childless. They desperately wanted children. In 1912, Mrs. Marland asked her sister if they could bring the two oldest children to Oklahoma to live with them.

Like orphans on the "Orphan Train," George and Lyde traveled west on the rails, but they were in the private railroad care of their uncle, E. W. Marland. Later the Marlands formally adopted the children.

"Lydie," as she wanted to be called, finished high school at St.

Mary's Catholic School in Ponca City. After graduation, she went to several finishing schools back east. During vacations, she came home to Ponca City to join in the social activities of the young people–swimming, dancing and riding horseback, her favorite activity.

Marland ordered the casting of two statues, one of Lydie and the other of her brother, to be placed in the garden at the Marland home. When he talked of his daughter, he used terms like beautiful, charming and graceful.

In June, 1926, Marland's wife died. She had been an invalid for some years. Two years later, Marland asked a judge to annul Lydie's adoption. They married in her birth parents' home in Flourtown on July 14, 1928.

Tabloids across the country picked up the story, calling it the "scandal that shocked the nation"—the idea of a 54-year-old millionaire marrying his 28-year-old niece and former adopted daughter! (263)

The oil man began construction of a mansion in her honor–$2.5 million, 55 rooms, including several ballrooms and 12 bathrooms. They moved into the new house immediately following a honeymoon trip to Canada and California. The sculptures were placed in the gardens surrounding the mansion for all to see.

Marland lost everything in 1928 when J. P. Morgan purchased more than enough shares of stock in Marland Oil to take control of the company. Marland was given a choice of being a figurehead official or leaving the company. He chose to leave.

Within two years, Marland and his young wife had to close the mansion and move into the guest house on the grounds in order to cut their monthly expenses. Marland never recouped his losses.

In 1932 he was elected to Congress. They moved to Washington, D.C.

Marland ran for governor in 1934 against a large field of candidates. He won. Lydie became Oklahoma's first lady on January 14, 1935.

A shy, introspective person by nature, Lydie was uncomfortable with the publicity. Perhaps the negative news stories of her adoption and marriage contributed to that perspective. But she performed her duties admirably. Many times they opened the mansion in Ponca City for state parties and affairs. Celebrities, such as Will Rogers, and other western entertainers, often spent weekends with them at the mansion, which they called the Palace on the Prairie. (264)

When his term as governor ended, the couple moved back to the guest house. He died on October 3, 1941, shortly after selling the mansion to the Discalced Carmelite Fathers of Mexico. Although Lydie was overwhelmed with grief, she continued to live in the guest house, which had not been sold. She did not engage in any of the town's social affairs, and many assumed she had died.

She asked Glen Gilchrist, a monument company owner, to destroy the sculpture of herself.

"Smash the face first," she told him. (265) She watched him strike the first blow. When she left, he buried the 760 pieces, without doing any more harm to the statue.

By 1953, Lydie had had enough of the constant stares and whisperings of people in Ponca City. She hit the road, not telling anyone of her destination. Police and private detectives searched for her in vain. Once a year, a check for the taxes on the cottage arrived at the Kay County treasurer's office. Every return postmark was from a different town.

In 1975 Lydie returned to Ponca City as quietly as she had departed. She received a small subsistence annuity from Conoco, the company formed when Morgan merged Marland Oil with Continental Oil Company. Moving back into the cottage, she remained a recluse, frail and poverty-stricken, for twelve more years. She purchased clothing at the Salvation Army. A neighbor occasionally looked in on her. She died friendless and alone in a Ponca City nursing home on July 28, 1987. Her schoolgirl devotion to her religious faith, the only remaining anchor in her life, sustained her in the final years.

Residents of Ponca City voted a special sales tax to buy the Marland Mansion. With matching funds from Conoco, they purchased the estate and opened it to public tours.

Gilchrist's family found the pieces of Lydie's statue, where he had buried them so many years before. They donated the broken limestone to the mansion commission, who had it restored. When workers reconstructed the head, the fragments fit together perfectly. It left a double line that resembled a tear, streaming down and across her Venus-like face. The restored sculpture is now on display in the foyer of the mansion.

In July, 1999, Lydie's cottage was opened to public tours. Her tragic private life made her a public figure after all.

While Lydie was struggling to find herself, there were other events transpiring that had an impact on the course of adoption in Oklahoma.

Women's Clubs and Dependent Children

During the 1930s, members of the Oklahoma's General Federation of Women's Clubs lobbied for better placements for dependent children. A small group toured a girls' reformatory in 1932, when Mrs. J. Hale Edwards of Lawton, the state president, saw a 10-year-old girl, playing with a doll in the corner of a room. (266)

She asked the matron what action the little girl could have possibly done to be sent to a state reformatory. Orphanages are full, she was told. The judge had nowhere else to send her. And what's more, the matron said, 10 to 20 percent of their incarcerated juveniles were in the same situation.

Mrs. Edwards was horrified that any child could be sent to a reformatory with older children, who were already exhibiting criminal behavior. She and the other ladies lobbied the governor for a ban on the courts, preventing judges from sending non-criminal children in state care to reformatories. Governor Murray promised to do something about it, but he never did. The women pressured succeeding governors for a policy change. It was a case of too many children for too few beds in the children's homes. The practice was not banned until the 1940s.

Governor William H. Murray "Alfalfa Bill"

The Depression didn't make Governor Murray a miser. It was part of his nature. He fanatically cut corners wherever he could, because he believed government should not be so big as to intrude into citizens' lives or their pocketbooks. He plowed the lawn surrounding the governor's mansion and planted potatoes. He cut salaries of state employees and sometimes refused to pay them for work they had already done.

There was no cohesive state child welfare program in Oklahoma during Murray's tenure. Mothers' pensions, which were doled out by county judges, were the only government funding for children to stay in their own homes. Each county was allocated $8,000, which fell far short of the needed funds.

Black Market Babies

Mabel Bassett, commissioner of Charities and Corrections, flexed the muscle of her office when a baby market scam broke into the news in 1933 with the headline, "Doctors Accused of Selling Babies." (267)

Three Tulsa physicians were accused of arranging payment plans for four adoptive couples of newborn babies. The amounts ranged from $70 to $100. The money was said to cover medical care and hospitalization. Helen Schaeffer, director of Tulsa's Children's Service Bureau, alerted Bassett to the cases, after she received phone calls from the adoptive parents, asking for information about the birth families.

Bassett immediately launched an investigation, because she considered the payments to be buying and selling the infants. However, there was no state statute prohibiting the practice.

Even the *New York Times* reported on the situation. "It's the state's shame that these cases can't be prosecuted. We need legislation badly to protect unfortunate girls," they wrote. (268)

The Tulsa World printed Mrs. Bassett's comments after she interviewed the three doctors.

They didn't even stop to realize that they were engaging in a slavery and taking every unfair advantage of poverty-stricken young girls who were unfortunate enough to be caught in such domestic predicaments....they were more interested in exacting their money from the foster parents than they were in determining whether the foundlings would have adequate care. (269)

Bassett said two of the babies were not placed with appropriate foster parents, but she could not remove the children from the homes, because of lax adoption laws. (270)

Blocked by state statute from doing anything about the arrangement, she had another idea. A *Tulsa Tribune* article told the tale. Bassett's office inspected all maternity and lying-in hospitals in the state. She said she would knock points off the inspection record of any hospital in the state that engaged in any form of child placement.

"Hospitals are not in the child-placing business. There are child-placing bureaus," Mrs. Bassett said. (271)

While Bassett was commissioner (1923-1947), the legislature refused to pass any bill that would prohibit hospitals, doctors, or other individuals from facilitating adoptions for profit.

State Orphanages

Some families, who didn't have enough food to eat, placed their children in one of the state's orphanages. These parents thought that the state would take care of their kids until they could earn enough to reclaim them. On occasion, because of the poverty level of parents, county officials committed the children without the agreement of the biological parents.

In one case, a birth father filed suit against the Whitaker Orphan Home of the State of Oklahoma, asking for custody of his six-year-old daughter. The little girl had been committed to the orphanage in 1935. She was placed with a couple, who had applied to be adoptive parents. The father alleged his daughter's custody had been obtained by fraud. The district court found the father's suit to be without merit. They didn't return the child.

The Daily Oklahoman published the following comments:

The suit is considered important because, if it had been decided against the state, hundreds of adoptions from state orphanages would have been thrown into dispute...Under state law, orphanage officials do not have to tell natural parents of children where they are sent. (272)

FERA in Oklahoma

The Federal Emergency Relief Agency (FERA) funneled federal dollars into Oklahoma to help the state's unemployed poor. Social workers, such as Dove Montgomery Kull, helped clients fill out the paperwork to receive the little dab of welfare that was available to them at the time. (273) Elderly, disabled or blind citizens could qualify for some assistance. Families could also access the system to a certain degree.

Governor Murray bristled at the idea of "hand-outs." A fight broke out between the Murray administration and the federal regulators of FERA. At issue was the educational level of caseworkers.

Federal administrators told the state that all funds would be cut off if social workers did not have college degrees.

State officials and legislators did not believe college was necessary for the job description. They wanted to be able to count years of experience in lieu of the college degree. The college graduates were labeled "sorority sisters." Newspaper headlines on a daily basis detailed the escalating verbal clashes over this issue and the whole relief effort. FERA funds were actually cut for a period of time.

Oklahomans began to look for a different answer to their economic problems. They knew Murray and his penny-pinching way wasn't going to solve the huge economic shortfall of so many individuals and families during the tough economic times.

Governor E. W. Marland

Voters elected E. W. Marland, a Ponca City oilman, to sort things out. And "sort out" he did—or he tried to. (274)

Marland's sister, Mrs. Ignatia M. Rittenhouse, a social worker in an eastern city, came to the state to survey its social problems. After visiting one poverty-stricken neighborhood, she said

The whole district should be burned...The health department of any large city would not permit such filth...Where is FERA?...Where is the social service exchange? (275)

Marland pushed the 1935 legislature into approving a bill that formed the Department of Public Welfare (DPW). This would allow social workers to access Social Security funds to serve old age pensioners, blind and disabled individuals, and dependent children.

The Public Welfare Commission (PWC) appointed Marland's personal attorney, Harve L. Melton, as director of the department to actually hire employees and lay the foundation for the new state agency. (276) State officials continued to squabble over the qualifications of social workers.

The Division of Child Welfare (DCW) was put into place when voters approved Oklahoma's Social Security Act in July, 1936.

In February, 1937, Melton appointed Laura Dester, a visiting teacher employed by the Indian Service at Fort Washakie, Wyoming, as head of the new DCW. Dester was originally from Deer Creek, a small town in Grant County, Oklahoma, just west of Ponca City, Marland's hometown. She exchanged the job of counseling and teaching English to Indian teenagers for the job of organizing and administering a whole new child welfare unit. Her educational background consisted of a bachelor's degree from Bethel College in Newton, Kansas, a Mennonite school, and fourteen hours of graduate work at the University of Chicago. Only two of those hours pertained to child welfare. Her other classes were in English and speech.

Child welfare's first priority was Aid to Dependent Children. In October, 1936, 10,305 families received $2.00 a child per month. No children were adopted through child welfare at that time. The commissioner of Charities and Corrections, county judges, lawyers, and social service agencies continued to handle all adoptions.

Adopted children were in a legal no man's land. There was no amended birth certificate that identified the adoptive parents as "parents." If the adoptive parents died without a will, the adoptees could not inherit anything from them. In 1935, State Representative James Nance (D-Walters), a newspaper editor and publisher, sponsored legislation to correct this problem. (277) The inheritance was to be based upon the adoption petition and the decree. The bill failed to pass.

Oklahoma Courts

Clarence J. Blinn, a former mayor of Oklahoma City, was appointed to replace County Judge C. C. Christison, who died of a sudden heart attack in his office in December, 1935. Perhaps Blinn was appointed because of his tall and gaunt appearance, resembling Abraham Lincoln. Or maybe it was because he lost his position as mayor through a political maneuver. Whatever the reason, the appointment began a judicial career that spanned 40 years.

Blinn handled most of the juvenile and adoption cases in Oklahoma County. An article in *The Daily Oklahoman* announced Blinn approved six adoptions in one day on January 4, 1936. Most adoptions come before Christmas, Blinn said, but this year, we have had more adoptions since Christmas. (278)

Like Christison, Blinn used the newspaper to facilitate adoptions. In November, 1936, two brothers, ages one and two, needed a home. The *Oklahoma City Times's* "Service Man" wrote a story about the boys and their need for a home. (279) The father had abandoned the family and the mother was unable to care for all the children. She wanted the youngest two boys to be adopted. Thirty-eight prospective adoptive couples applied. Blinn wrote a letter to the editor, thanking him for his help.

Choosing from so many couples was difficult, Blinn said, but he was gratified with the response from so many couples:

> Human hearts still throb and willing hands still reach out to aid the helpless…Every application was deserving. But there were so many of them. As a last resort, we tried our level best to adjust these babies into that home into which it seemed they might have been born. (280)

The last sentence of the article said, "The boys are the sons for all time of a splendid young Oklahoma City couple." (281)

Legislative Lobbies

Every group wanted a piece of Oklahoma's tight financial budget.

O. J. Fox, a Corporation Commission official and part-time radio preacher, created the Oklahoma Social Welfare Association (OSWA) to solicit monthly dues of $2 each from his elderly listeners. The money was to be used to lobby Oklahoma state legislators for increased benefits to senior citizens.

Oklahoma's elderly liked Fox and believed he could help them secure increased assistance payments.

Fox's lobbying efforts created extra pressure on the state legislature to curtail spending for children, so more money could be dedicated to the elderly.

Teachers also lobbied the state legislature for increased salaries and aid to education, further reducing the funds available for children.

Delegations from various parts of the state fought for increased funding of state roads in their areas.

Even in the1930s, the list of lobbying groups was long. Few people were speaking for the rights of children.

Governor "Red" Phillips

"Red" Phillips campaigned long and hard for governor in 1938. His platform called for austerity in state government. Phillips vowed to clean up Marland's $41 million debt and balance the budget. (282) His speeches left the impression that Marland alone was responsible for frivolous spending while in office, even though the state had formed the Oklahoma Highway Patrol and the Department of Public Welfare during his administration. In addition, Oklahoma voters had elected to give every qualified elderly applicant $30 per month in pension benefits. Applications and the list of relief recipients ballooned. Newspapers printed the names of pension recipients. National social work leaders used the newspaper lists to expose Oklahoma's welfare system—and the numbers of ineligible elderly who were receiving aid. It began with an article in the social work journal, *Survey Graphic*. (283)

National Pressure

In April, 1938, Paul Kellogg's social work journal, *Survey Graphic*, published an article by associate editor Beulah Amidon, who complained that the small amount of aid given to Oklahoma's children, half the national average, was caused by a record of "ineptitude, political maneuvering, disregard of human needs and constitutes a real challenge to our democracy...Can we muster the men and women to put them (good policies and procedures) into effect?" (284)

Amidon believed elderly, ineligible individuals were receiving grants at the expense of Oklahoma's children. She said one hundred fifty-seven deceased elderly persons were getting government checks and many more unqualified recipients were receiving aid, because Oklahoma did not have a systematic age verification procedure in place.

Washington regulators were appalled at the lack of supervision in the program. A hearing was scheduled in Washington for Oklahoma officials to explain the number of elderly recipients, who did not have appropriate documentation of their need for relief. Federal grants-in-aid checks to Oklahoma were stopped.

Long-time legislator Jess Harper was appointed director to clean up the relief rolls. Social workers began reviewing all casework records to verify each recipient was entitled to aid—a painstaking process. In order for Oklahoma to have its federal welfare checks reinstated, all case records had to be reinvestigated. State legislators were under a tremendous amount of budgetary pressure to do whatever was required to keep the federal dollars flowing into the program.

Barely a month after Amidon's article appeared, the Children's Bureau published a booklet, entitled "Problems to be Considered in Legislation on Adoption as Illustrated by the Law of Selected States." While Oklahoma was being punished for lax record-keeping of elderly welfare recipients, federal Children's Bureau caseworkers were pushing for the confidentiality of adoption records:

Number 7. <u>Provision for changes to be made in birth records</u>. The birth record from which certificates of age are issued should bear the name that the child has been given upon adoption. This has been accomplished in a number of states by authorizing a change in the birth certificate at the time of adoption. Provisions for this is made in the adoption laws of Wisconsin, and Alabama; in a number of other States it is found in the vital statistics law.

Number 8. Confidential nature of adoption records. It should be noted that in all three States the files and records of the court in adoption proceedings are confidential and are not open to inspection. This is a very desirable procedure. (285)

Another Children's Bureau booklet, which was directly addressed to Oklahoma, told readers

In any revision of the adoption law, consideration should be given to additional provisions which would include a residence period in the adoption home prior to adoption, an investigation by the State Department or its representatives when the child is a minor, the confidential nature of adoption records and reports to the Bureau of Vital Statistics so that the child's birth record can be changed in accordance with his adoptive status. (286)

The handwriting on the wall was clear. The Children's Bureau believed Oklahoma should close its adoption records.

Sealing Original Birth Certificates

Election coverage filled the newspapers in the fall of 1938. In addition to the office of governor, voters were electing many state representatives. Creekmore Wallace, a lawyer representing the area around the state capitol, ran for re-election unopposed. Many of his constituents were state government employees, who were concerned about the state budget and their own paychecks.

Pressure mounted when the *Social Security Bulletin* published federal regulations, tying Social Security entitlement funding to the confidentiality of records. (287)

As soon as the 1939 legislative session opened, Wallace introduced a bill to seal all original birth certificates and issue amended birth certificates with the adoptive parents' names substituted for the birth parents. Later in the week, he filed a special resolution that stripped Mabel Bassett of any legislative funding for the office of commissioner of Charities and Corrections. Even though the resolution failed to pass, it effectively derailed any attempt Bassett might have made to fight for adoptive children to have access to their own records. She had to spend her time fighting for her own department's survival.

There was no other organized opposition to the sealed records' bill. Legislators were anxious to find adoptive homes for the many children who were receiving foster care benefits. After the bill passed on February 10, 1939, a state senator told a *Daily Oklahoman* reporter that birth certificates were sealed, and new birth certificates issued, so "adoptive parents wouldn't feel embarrassed when they enrolled their children in school." (288)

Later that spring, when DPW social workers finished re-vamping all the case files and closed its records, Social Security restored the federal grants-in-aid payments to Oklahoma. Child welfare workers began to facilitate adoptions—and the Health Department sealed adoptees' original birth certificates.

The *Social Work Yearbook for 1939* made Oklahoma an example for all other states, by publicizing the cancellation of federal money until all administrative deficiencies were cleared and the records were closed. (289)

Two Adoption Decisions

Two additional decisions involving Oklahoma adoptions were made in 1939.

Roy J. Turner, a future state governor, was running for election to the Oklahoma City school board. Although Turner was a wealthy oilman and owned a huge cattle ranch in southern Oklahoma, he had no children. The Turners applied for a child to adopt. Seven-year-old twins, Bill and Betty, were placed with them for adoption. Born at the Home of Redeeming Love in 1932, the twins had been adopted by another couple. For unknown reasons, the adoption fell through. The children were re-adopted by the Turners. (290)

Mae Marshall and her husband also applied to various social agencies for a baby. Every one rejected them. Angry at being spurned as an adoptive mother, she contacted the *Oklahoma City Times*, urging an article be written that would condemn agencies and social workers for not allowing her to adopt. She told the reporter they were turned down because of age. Marshall said they were both 40, but she was 44 and her husband was 51 at the time. The article, with a picture of herself and the layette she purchased for her prospective adopted child, appeared in the *Oklahoma City Times* on May 20, 1939. (291)

Oklahoma had not heard the last of Mae Marshall.

CHAPTER 13

CHILDREN'S ISSUES IN THE LEGISLATURE

While most Oklahoma's children spent their leisure time playing baseball and going to Saturday afternoon movies, economically deprived children continued to flood orphanages and social service agencies during the 1940s. Many parents could not afford to feed their children. One choice was to deposit them in an orphanage until the family's finances improved. For some parents, getting on their feet was a pipe dream that would never happen.

Legislators and orphanage directors began to look at adoption as an option for those children, so more beds would be available for kids who were recently placed in state custody.

In other cases, children of single mothers were placed in foster care, funded by county and state taxpayers. World War II and society's mobility added to the number of women who became instant "grass widows." These were mothers who received aid, while keeping their children at home. Legislators wanted to find a way to share the burden of paying for the care of these children.

Newspapers continued to tout adoption plans. An *Oklahoma City Times'* columnist, called "The Service Man," reported babies were much in demand by prospective adoptive parents. (292)

Two stories highlighted the need for adoptive children. A Minco couple wanted a baby not more than three months old. The prospective adoptive mother said the baby would have the "best of care and a mother's love." (293)

A Union City farmer wanted a boy and a girl. They would be expected to work for their board and room. The girl would milk one cow and help with the cooking. The boy would work on the farm. (294)

The articles said the prospective adoptive parents would furnish references.

Mabel Bassett didn't think that was enough. The commissioner of Charities and Corrections believed judges should make a thorough investigation of each prospective adoptive couple, and infants should be observed in foster care to find any abnormalities, which would make placement in an adoptive home difficult.

Bassett was a warrior and a force for justice in Oklahoma. From 1923, when she was elected state commissioner of Charities and Corrections, she battled everyone, from state legislators to county sheriffs to district attorneys—always keeping in mind her duty to protect children and families.

The ink had hardly dried on the bill to establish amended birth certificates, when Bassett began talking to state legislators about requiring home studies for prospective adoptive parents. (295) She saw too many cases of children being placed with people whom she felt were unfit to be parents. If the state was going to seal the original birth certificates, it could at least make sure the new parents were suitable for the job at hand—caring for Oklahoma's newest citizens in a loving way. State law prevented birth parents–those divorced, in prison, or alcoholics–from giving any input into the court process regarding their children. It seemed unfair that prospective adoptive parents did not have the same scrutiny.

A bill designed to require home studies was introduced into the legislature in 1941, 1943, and 1945. Each time, it failed. Bassett never saw her efforts bear fruit, while she was in office.

After 23 years as commissioner of Charities and Corrections, her popularity began to wane. In the 1946 primary election, she garnered more votes than anyone else within a field of eight candidates, but she did not have a majority. Forced into a run-off, she campaigned hard against former highway patrolman Buck Cook. It wasn't enough. Insiders attributed Bassett's defeat to the animosity created by her sweeping investigations of jails, orphanages, and other state institutions. (296)

In the governor's race, oilman, rancher and adoptive parent Roy Turner ran against attorney William O. Coe. During campaign speeches, Coe talked extensively about juvenile problems and the child welfare court he envisioned.

"A mother with strong convictions and a broad understanding of social problems should run it, without consideration of whether she may or may not be a lawyer," Coe said. (297) Apparently, protecting a child's legal rights was not important to the candidate. No one knows how Turner felt. There is no record of his response to the remarks.

During this period, Oklahoma's child welfare system did not

provide support for pregnant women who were over the age of majority.

While Buck Cook prepared to take over as commissioner of Charities and Corrections, the Children's Bureau and the federal Department of Labor sent a legal opinion to the state attorney general's office and the Division of Child Welfare, informing them that every pregnant woman—regardless of age—was to receive aid if she was economically disadvantaged. The federal government based that opinion on the fact that every deprived pregnant woman should be given aid, because it was for the welfare of the child. (298)

As a result, pressure within state government mounted to find ways to take care of the burgeoning number of pregnant women whose infants could not be cared for in their own homes.

One cynical state official, Maude R. Calvert, noted "too many relatives are shunting elderly persons and half-orphaned children off as state wards, when they could be kept at home." (299)

Private maternity homes and voluntary agencies expanded to help meet the needs of unmarried mothers.

Mae Marshall, who was boarding pregnant women in her home, began to send her maternity cases to the new Edmond Hospital for delivery. Prospective adoptive parents picked up the babies directly from the hospital, making payments for foster care unnecessary. Mabel Bassett was not in office to ensure points were knocked off hospital inspection records. The prospective adoptive parents were instructed to have their own attorney file the adoption petition in the county where they were living at the time of the adoption. Birth mothers signed the relinquishment forms at the Oklahoma County courthouse in the courtroom of County Judge

Clarence J. Blinn.

Social welfare advocates again lobbied the state legislature to pass a bill requiring the investigation of homes of prospective adoptive parents. Representative Walter Billingsley, "Baby Doe's" adoptive father, sponsored the measure in the state House of Representatives in 1947. (300) One version of the bill prohibited the "sale" of babies. Maternity homes, hospitals, agencies, or individuals would not be able to accept compensation from the adoptive parents. Another section said agencies could not offer adoption as an inducement for a woman to enter a home for maternity care.

A number of individuals and agencies lobbied against the measure.

"This bill (Billingsley's house bill) sets up a division of snoopers who will pry into the private affairs of every person who seeks to adopt a baby," George Campbell (D-Sand Springs) shouted on the house floor. (301)

Catholic Charities's head, the Rt. Rev. James A. Garvey, also blasted the measure in an editorial published in the *Southwest Courier*, the weekly Catholic newspaper. He said many states were looking at revising their adoption codes, and federal regulators were looking on with interest. Garvey reminded readers the federal government had withheld funds from Oklahoma in the 1930s because it refused to take orders regarding its own state affairs. He continued,

In opposing this proposed legislation, we are not bitter…we are simply defending our religious and civil rights. We wish to be free to do the work God has given us to do, for which we have been educated and trained, and in which we have had over 20 years' experience... (302)

The *Oklahoma City Times* published a whole page feature, headlined, "Stamping Out the 'Sale' of Babies." (303) The main thrust of the article was to warn prospective adoptive parents that buying a baby from an independent baby broker could bring them emotional heartache. A congenital defect in the baby could affect their happiness with the child.

> Only one fourth of the states have adoption laws that approximate the standards believed to be necessary for adequate protection of the children, natural parents and adoptive parents. (304)

Oklahoma was not one of them. In fine print, under the picture of several available babies, the caption read

> Careful placement of these babies in properly investigated homes gives them a good chance to share in the advantages available to more fortunate youngsters. (305)

Billingsley's bill passed the House. The Senate subcommittee voted to approve the measure. It was sent to the floor with a 'do pass' recommendation. However, a group of senators who despised social workers immediately filed a substitute measure.

Edith Johnson, a *Daily Oklahoman* columnist, wrote that the coalition of rebel senators believed Billingsley's bill was communistic and written by a bunch of "political bobbysoxers." (306)

The sticking point for the senators appeared to be the home studies. It's been needlessly alleged that the investigations of prospective adoptive parents is connected to the investigations of persons applying for old age pensions, Johnson wrote. "Why anybody would make such an allegation is not easy to comprehend." (307)

The revised measure allowed the county judges to order a home study at the request of the adoptive parents—as if those parents would call for an investigation of themselves! (308) It banned the sale of babies, as well as making all adoption records confidential, except upon court order. (309)

On the Senate floor, social workers were accused of "lacking in the milk of human kindness, with being "do-gooders," "busy-bodies" and being overly zealous. (310)

Legislators had not forgotten the headline-grabbing case of a kidnapped ten-month-old baby girl from a foster home in Oklahoma City.

Initially, Child Welfare director Laura Dester believed the baby to be stolen by someone, who planned to offer the child for adoption on the black market.

Upon investigation, it was learned the birth mother and three other individuals had taken the baby. Mother and child were found at the baby's previous foster home in Tulsa. The foster parents had paid a private investigator to find the baby because they wanted to adopt the baby themselves. Child Welfare contended they had obtained permanent custody of the baby through a Tulsa County court order. The birth mother complained the social worker had illegally taken the baby from her.

Until 1997, Oklahoma law said a birth mother had thirty days to change her mind after she signed a relinquishment form. Birth mothers believed their child would automatically be returned to them. It was a lie. What social workers and lawyers did not tell birth mothers was that, if they wanted to revoke the relinquishment, a court hearing would be scheduled. A judge would then determine what was in the child's "best interest." Judges could use the fact that a birth mother signed a relinquishment as a reason the birth mother would not make an appropriate home for the baby. No one thought about changing the statute to correct this abuse of the law.

The case was appealed to the Oklahoma State Supreme Court. While the baby was returned to the birth mother, the Oklahoma State Supreme Court justices did not publish their ruling. It could not be used as precedent.

Streeter Speakman, the birth mother's attorney, told a reporter

No one says that the mother is unfit or incapable of caring for her own child. No one claims that the State of Oklahoma needs the child. The State of Oklahoma just wants to appease a pampered pride that finds birth in a false self-appraisal of the importance of the Department of Public Welfare, the broken heart of a mother notwithstanding. (311)

As a result of the legislative bickering and innuendos about the professionalism of social workers, Billingsley's original bill mandating home studies, as well as the substitute Senate measure, died.

Mae Marshall's Private Home for Unfortunate Girls and other adoption-related agencies continued business as usual. Classified ads were placed daily in the "personal" section of local newspapers for prospective adoptive parents, as well as for pregnant women who needed maternity confinement.

Many state legislators liked private maternity home care, because it lessened the caseload for Laura Dester and DCW— fewer state dollars would be funneled into the "unwed mother" problem. It made foster care unnecessary because adoptive parents took the babies directly from the hospital.

While some legislators called social workers "bobbysoxers" and "sorority sisters," Laura Dester called them her halo, or golden, girls. They worked long hours, trying to make a difference in the lives of every neglected child in the State of Oklahoma. As soon as abandoned or abused children came to the attention of the welfare department, social workers were expected to immediately find foster homes for them, without the benefit of any list from which to draw. It was imperative they have a good relationship with community leaders, who would be available to help establish a plan for the care of these unfortunate children.

Longtime social worker Deborah Rothe wrote:

Laura expected her workers to stand on their own two feet. She accepted no excuse for failing to get what a child needed. She further expected her workers to keep the community abreast of problems in the field. Political astuteness was perhaps her greatest asset. (312)

During the 1940s, five child welfare demonstration projects expanded to 14 districts, serving all seventy-seven counties. Applications from prospective adoptive families were received from all over the state. If an unwed mother decided to place her child for adoption through DCW, the baby was placed in foster care in Oklahoma County. A physical and psychological evaluation determined the level of development an adoptive family could expect. A background investigation of the birth family was made. Dester wrote that the home studies were necessary to place the child in the home that would be best suited to his or her needs. (313)

Hidden among the papers at the Oklahoma State Archives is a case study of a birth mother, written by Laura Dester.

Carolyn's parents are financially secure and well-respected in the community. Carolyn had just told them of her problem. They immediately went to their family physician for guidance. Carolyn was 19 and had been away from home for her first year of college. There, she met the father of her unborn child. Disturbed and distressed as Carolyn's parents were about her, they recognized that they must consider the unborn child as well. The understanding physician listened. He recognized her problem. His counsel had been asked and he gave it. The parents are financially secure and had never faced a situation requiring services of a social agency. Arrangements were made for Carolyn to meet the child welfare worker. It took time and skill on the part of the worker to obtain Carolyn's cooperation. She had brought her parents trouble and her feeling of guilt and utter state of helplessness created only confusion in her mind. The worker understood Carolyn's dilemma. It was not too long until Carolyn realized that she, too, must focus on the unborn child. She gained new incentive to live when she recognized this and accepted responsibility. She realized that by doing her part, she would give the child a better opportunity to be well-born. Foster home care in an urban center was obtained for Carolyn and she had excellent prenatal care. When the baby was born, Carolyn had reached her decision. She had confidence in the child welfare worker and in the Division of Child Welfare to select for her child a home, which would give her infant son the care and protection to which he was entitled. Carolyn returned to school. Her experience, tragic as it was, has not left her bitter. (314)

In the post-World War II era, the stigma of being an unwed

mother, coupled with the illegitimate status of the baby, placed a burden of prejudice upon both the mother and child. Because of public opinion, unmarried mothers from middle class parents almost never kept their babies.

During the1949 legislative session, social welfare activists again introduced adoption legislation, which would have required licenses for maternity homes, commercial placement of babies would have been outlawed and adoption records at the courthouse would have been sealed. (315) The measure failed.

As time marched on from the 1940s into the 1950s, politicians and businessmen had other issues on their minds.

Route 66, the "Mother Road" of the West and Midwest, connected Oklahoma City and Tulsa (T-town). While the capitol building graced Oklahoma City, T-Town was home to a number of oil companies. Anyone who often traveled the road complained loudly and long about the time it took to traverse the 90 miles over the hilly, two-lane road. A four-lane toll road would expedite commerce between the two cities.

Tulsa legislators used their muscle at the capitol to further their goals. Funds were approved to widen Route 66 into a toll road in 1947. Construction began immediately.

Named after Governor Roy J. Turner, the four-lane Turner Turnpike opened on May 16, 1953. Politicians, oilmen, and truckers sped up and down the new toll road. And so did the babies of unmarried mothers. It was not a secret within the welfare department that babies born in Tulsa would be adopted in Oklahoma City. And Oklahoma City babies would be adopted in Tulsa.

As the Aid to Dependent Children (ADC) rolls skyrocketed,

pressure mounted within the state budget. A reporter at a Tulsa newspaper, writing under the pseudonym Investigator X, penned an editorial and a five-part series, blaming unmarried mothers for Oklahoma's budget problems. "Under the Guise of Welfare—Oklahoma Breeding a Society of Illegitimates and Chiselers," the headline read. (316)

The inflammatory articles said that idle, unmarried parents were getting tax dollars to feed their illegitimate children. Lloyd Rader, the new DHS director, and other political figures worked on plans to "fix" the problem. Unmarried mothers must not be allowed to keep their children. Recruiting adoptive homes became a priority.

On August 31, 1951, *The Tulsa Tribune* publicized a reunion between a birth mother and her 21-year-old birth son, who had been adopted as a toddler. Kidnapped from Pampa, Texas, when he was nineteen months old, the toddler was later found on a Tulsa street and adopted. The birth mother said she spent years searching for him. "Thursday was the first time I had heard his voice in about 18 years." (317)

The adoptive father claimed the birth mother's story was false during an interview for the very next edition of the *Tribune*.

While the boy's father did abandon the toddler in Tulsa, "(the birth mother) has known all along where the boy was," the adoptive father told a reporter. (318)

The story scared state officials. If birth mothers were going to search for their long-lost children, it would be more difficult to find adoptive parents. Legislators began to consider closing the court records as well as the original birth certificates.

Johnston Murray, Alfalfa Bill Murray's son, was elected

governor. On February 7, 1952, he issued his weekly newsletter, which was sent to all the newspapers in the state. The subject was what to do about unmarried mothers and their children:

What should be the state's official attitude toward illegitimate children? An Oklahoma physician, with considerable experience treating unmarried mothers, asks the question. He contends there must be closer supervision of husbandless families, citing the following examples as proof of a breakdown in the accepted moral code.

One girl has an illegitimate pregnancy, which in itself is not unusual, but I was surprised at her attitude. I asked what she intended to do and suggested a talk with the man responsible.

Her reply was, 'That's no cause for worry. A girl friend of mine said I would get $40 immediately from welfare.'

A second case, among several listed by the doctor, is equally disturbing. This one involves a girl who has had two illegitimate children and is receiving the usual welfare help. She now has another illegitimate pregnancy and is utterly unconcerned. She merely states her boyfriend is the father, and that is that. She is anticipating help for her third child.

SOLUTIONS SCARCE: The doctor admits he doesn't have any sure-fire solutions to the above outlined problem. But he points out there are states, which give aid for only the first illegitimate child. I am in complete accord with the doctor's view that such cases require very close supervision. However, I question the wisdom of trying to reduce illegitimacy by passing a law against it.

True, refusing state aid would be certain and severe punishment for the mother. It would be equally severe and unjust punishment of helpless children. I don't believe any reasonable person is so callous as to want that. (319)

Adoption seemed to be the best way to keep children from becoming permanent wards of the state. Sealing the court records and giving total confidentiality to the adoptive parents could encourage more people to become adoptive parents.

Fourteen years had passed since the legislature sealed the original birth certificates and replaced them with the amended birth certificates, showing the adoptive parents to be the only parents of the adopted person. As teenagers, these young people would soon have the opportunity to check their own court files. That point was not lost on state legislators. The bill to seal all adoption-related court files was signed into law by Governor Johnston Murray on March 24, 1953.

Sealed records can hide a multitude of problems—not the least of which is the fact that the state legislature continued to refuse to pass a law mandating home studies for prospective adoptive parents.

Our next chapter outlines how Mae Marshall became Oklahoma's most flamboyant maternity home operator.

CHAPTER 14

A THRIVING MATERNITY HOME

Oklahoma's most notorious maternity home, Mae Marshall's Private Home for Unfortunate Girls, began as the cottage industry of a bored housewife, looking for something to do with her time. As the business expanded, utility buildings called "chicken coops" were installed in the backyard to provide more bed space. Eventually, Marshall was charged with trafficking in children, but never convicted in any court of law. The court of public opinion, however, was an entirely different matter.

The following story is reconstructed from public records and newspaper stories. It depicts Mae's entry into the world of adoption and the development of her maternity home.

*   *   *

Mae Marshall wanted a baby–a little girl. She was lonely during the day when her boys were in school. Evenings were spent with baseball and homework. Her husband Harry worked in the oil field—first, in Chickasha, Oklahoma, and then in El Dorado, Kansas. What was a body to do for companionship?

As soon as the boys were off to school, she poured herself a cup of coffee and sat down with the newspaper. Scanning the paper, she saw stories of unwanted babes. The Home of Redeeming Love advertised babies for adoption. Other advertisers were the Fairmont Hospital in Kansas City, Missouri, and Oklahoma City's Maternal Aid Guild operated by J. G. Bailey, D.O.

She placed her coffee mug on the table and tilted her head back against the chair. She sighed. Her whole body shook.

"So many unwanted children!" she exclaimed aloud to an empty kitchen. "Just yesterday at the grocery store, there was a young woman with two little ones and she didn't have enough money to purchase the milk her children needed. It's unfair!"

She closed her eyes, daydreaming and reminiscing about her life. She was born in Gilmer, Texas, on November 29, 1895, the third daughter of William N. and Theodocia (Kelly) Puckett. Named Jessie Mae, she guessed her parents had wanted a boy. Shortly after her birth, her mother became pregnant again and delivered a baby brother, Jessie. When their father died in 1905, Uncle Jessie, her mother's brother, moved in with them.

Life in east Texas was difficult in the early 1900s. Only wealthy town people had indoor plumbing and electricity. Sweet potatoes were the main cash crop. Lumberjacks only recently began a tiny logging industry. Underground oil reserves were undiscovered and untapped. Uncle Jessie worked for the Texas Rangers. Mae remembered his stories of families who were too poor to keep their children. On the other side of the tracks stood a black orphanage, called the Dickson Home.

Even when Mae was little, she always cried when she remembered those children, who didn't have parents who loved them.

As a teenager, Mae fell head-over-heels for a school chum named Guy Cates. They married. She gave birth to a baby boy, Willie Loutrell Cates, on her birthday in 1913. The infant died March 21, 1914. Medical care was scarce in the backwoods of Texas.

Guy and Mae had two more boys, Rex and John Douglas Cates. They moved to Tulsa, where Guy was hired as a painter for the Tulsa Public Schools. Mae worked in a grocery store, where she observed many young mothers without enough money to adequately feed their children. Eventually, Mae and Guy Cates divorced.

Mae married an oil field worker named Harry C. Marshall from West Virginia. The new couple bought a home on the south side of the Capitol Hill area in Oklahoma City. It was a happy time—until Harry left for Chickasha to work in the oil field. Mae was depressed and felt ill. The doctor told her to find an activity she was interested in.

Mae's head whipped to attention. She wanted a baby! That was a real interest!

She grabbed the phone and called the Home of Redeeming Love. They told her that she and Harry were too old to adopt.

"Too old?" Mae was livid. Her hands clutched a rag, as she scoured the kitchen floor, muttering obscenities about the Home.

Harry told her to try some other places. He said he was sure she would find a baby!

When she called the other adoption agencies, they also turned her down. An employee in the state's Child Welfare Department said they didn't do adoptions.

The capillaries in Mae's face swelled, making angry red blotches. She knew she would be a wonderful mother—if they'd only give her a chance. She called a reporter at the *Oklahoma City Times* to complain that she was denied a baby based on age discrimination. They printed the story. (320)

She called several area physicians, who were known to have large maternity practices. She interviewed every available married expectant mother, who was thinking about giving up her child. She named all the advantages that she and her husband could give a baby. Five different couples considered giving their baby to Mae and Harry. Once the babies were born, however, they changed their minds.

"What do I have to do to get a baby?" Mae cried.

One young couple seemed especially promising. The girl was impressed with the layette Mae had purchased for the baby. Labor began and the girl entered Capitol Hill Hospital. Mae paced the floor in the hallway outside the delivery room. As soon as the baby was born, the nurse brought her to Mae. She was perfect. Ten pink toes and ten tiny fingers. Curly black hair framed the baby's forehead. Mae was ecstatic and proud. She was going to be a mother to a little girl!

A photographer from the *Oklahoma City Times* took pictures of Mae and the baby for publication. (321)

She called everyone in her family to share the news. Then she telephoned the birth mother's mother. "It's a beautiful baby. Wouldn't you like to come and see her?" The grandmother rushed to the nursery. As soon as she saw the baby, she thought the newborn looked just like her daughter. She began to talk to her daughter about the possibility of keeping the child. When the couple decided not to relinquish the baby, Mae was devastated. Her hopes had been smashed again.

Winter turned into spring and Mae's arms continued to be empty. "Maybe if I offered them a place to live, that would encourage them!" she thought.

Mae contacted county health nurses, pharmacists and others who might come in contact with expectant mothers. The telephone began to ring and ring. Women who were pregnant and destitute began to find their way to Mae's door. She gave one girl and then another a place to stay while awaiting the birth of their babies.

Most birth mothers were still confused about what they wanted to do. But one young birth mother was positive that Mae would be her baby's mother. The prospective adoptive mother talked to the doctor, impressing him that the birth mother and her family should not see the baby. "I won't let a grandmother pull the rug out from under me again!" she exclaimed.

After the baby was born, the smiling adoptive couple carried the baby to the car. Now Harry and Mae would have a baby who belonged to both of them. Harry drove, as he chatted with Mae about their bundle of joy. Dressed in pink, the adorable baby filled Mae's thoughts with love.

As soon as Harry dropped Mae and the baby off at the house, he had to go back to work. Mae could not hold her often enough. The infant's heart-shaped mouth melted Mae's own heart. She was energized by the needs of this tiny little thing whom they called Norma Jean. Rex and Doug didn't mind taking a backseat to their new little sister. Mae told them it was only until she got big enough to help herself.

However, the telephone kept ringing. Pregnant girls were finding out about Mae and wanting a place to hide until they could go to the hospital. Mae hated to turn anyone away. "There are so many women out there, like me, who want another baby, and can't have one. Birth mothers don't need their babies. We have got to help these adoptive mothers get babies from the birth mothers, who can't take care of them, anyway," Mae told Harry. It also didn't hurt that the birth mothers could relieve Mae of the manual labor of cooking and cleaning.

Harry shook his head. "Whatever you want to do, Mae," he said quietly, fearing an outburst if he contradicted her opinion.

Harry and Mae adopted a second little girl.

In 1943, Mae looked north, to the Oklahoma City suburb called Edmond, Oklahoma. It was home to Central State College, renamed the University of Central Oklahoma, the state's first teacher's college. A ready supply of women in their child-bearing years who needed maternity help was available there.

Every weekend, Mae talked to Harry about Edmond. The Capitol Hill area of Oklahoma City was all right, but Saturday nights around the Redskin Theater was a rough part of town. Community camp wasn't far away. Groups of youngsters seemed to loiter everywhere. Mae didn't feel comfortable continuing to raise a family in south Oklahoma City.

Edmond was different. It was a family town. The landscape was dotted with churches and schools—and potential birth mothers.

Mae and Harry purchased a house on Ayres, just two blocks

west of the campus. Once there, Mae continued to talk to pregnant girls and women, and anyone else who might be in a position to persuade birth mothers to give up their children.

As her own adopted girls grew, the house became smaller and smaller, depending on the number of pregnant women who were staying with Mae. She began drinking to dull the pain of listening to never ending complaints about the cramped quarters. Ironically, a member of the Women's Christian Temperance Union lived in the neighborhood. In 1945, Mae and Harry purchased a house on the east side of the campus from Asia May Kessler, the mother of Edmond's mayor, John Kessler. She continued to drink.

The most difficult thing about Edmond, Mae believed, was that there was no hospital. The girls had to be transported to Oklahoma City for delivery. A funeral home provided taxi service for the girls to go to the hospital, but Mae couldn't depend on a driver to be available. If a hospital was in Edmond, she could call a local cab.

Mae talked to Doyle H. Fleetwood, M.D., who had recently established his medical practice in Edmond. Although Fleetwood was actually from Marlow, Oklahoma, he also had family in Longview, Texas, which was just down the road from Gilmer, Mae's hometown. Fleetwood listened intently to Mae's story. Caught up in the euphoria of helping pregnant women and babies, he enlisted two other physicians and a pharmacist to help him establish a full-service hospital in Edmond.

The physician met with C. H. Spearman, a businessman and the husband of a teacher in the Edmond Public Schools. The couple operated the Broncho Theater. They lived in an apartment on the second floor. The doctors thought the rooms would meet the hospital needs of a growing community.

Renovation work began in 1946. The hospital opened in February, 1947. Ironically, before the hospital opened, the Broncho Theater showed the film "Black Market Babies," produced by Monogram Pictures and starring Ralph Morgan and Jane Hazard. (322)

The audio portion of the movies could be heard overhead in the operating/delivery room. Doctors and other staff members mouthed the words of the movies, while they worked. By the end of each week, they had memorized the script of whatever movie was showing.

Because adoption requires legal documentation, Mae had to hire an attorney. She looked for a young attorney who had few clients. First, O. B. Martin filled the bill. He had been part of Roosevelt's Office of Price Administration during World War II. Later, attorney Forrest Simon stepped in to work with Mae. His wife Elizabeth told the author that they would have starved if it hadn't been for Mae Marshall. She gave them cans of green beans when they lacked the money to buy groceries.

When Mrs. Simon became pregnant, she was ill for most of the nine months of pregnancy. One of Mae's pregnant girls moved in with them to help Elizabeth with the housework and cooking.

Simon remained Mae's attorney until he couldn't justify her flippant attitude regarding legal records anymore, Mrs. Simon told the author. Edmond attorney, W. Custer Service, replaced him.

Mae's first classified ad in *The Daily Oklahoman* appeared in the personal section on August 1, 1948. She used the name Hope Cottage, mimicking a maternity home in Dallas. On October 3, her ad changed to "Mae Marshall's Private Home for Unfortunate Girls. Seclusion with expenses pd. Box 186. Edmond, Okla." (323)

She also took out an ad in the yellow pages of the Edmond telephone book.

Mae would talk to anyone about the wonderful service she was performing for women who found themselves in desperate and unwed circumstances.

No one could do more for these unfortunate women than I do, she told listeners. Where else could they go? I offer them a place to recuperate and have their babies. When they go back to their families, they will forget about the experience.

Mae was so sure of herself that she ignored the neighborhood gossip. Some people said Mae drank too much. Others commented on the Cadillacs she drove and the trips to Arkansas for horse racing. People wondered how she could afford such a lifestyle with only the small board fees paid by the adoptive parents.

All was not well in the Marshall home. When Mae learned about the Georgia Tann black market baby investigation in Memphis, Harry worried about its effect on Mae's business. He was tired of the whole thing. Mae filed for divorce. He moved out—another victim of her never-ending arrogance.

Mae prided herself on the widespread geographical distance of both the birth mothers and the adoptive parents who used her service. Birth mothers came from ten different states. Babies were placed in the homes of three states, primarily in Oklahoma, Texas and Louisiana.

Pregnant women spent much of their time walking around in the neighborhood, getting exercise, but also to get away from the cramped, stifling box-like atmosphere of the chicken coops where they were housed. Mae had purchased the small buildings from an Edmond lumberyard to expand the number of beds on her property.

The girls were required to do all the cooking and cleaning for Mae and her daughters. One birth mother talked about Mae's parrot. Her job was to clean the bird's cage. For some reason, the parrot didn't like to have his newspaper changed. When the birth mother approached the cage, he would scream, "Bitch! Bitch!" Mae always laughed hysterically.

She acted as if the birth mothers, and her adopted daughters, were her personal servants. When Mae was upset with her daughters, she told them they were required to do whatever she told them to do, because she was doing all this for them! What "all this" meant is only a matter of conjecture, because no one really knew.

Rumors of back-room adoption deals surfaced in 1954. Upset by innuendo, Fleetwood stopped delivering Mae's babies. She was forced to send girls back to the Capitol Hill Hospital in south Oklahoma City or to other area hospitals.

It was only the beginning of what was to come.

CHAPTER 15

SHERIFF'S KNOCK

A federal United States marshal knocked on Mae's front door one afternoon in June, 1955, with a subpoena for her to appear in Chicago before Estes Kefauver's Senate subcommittee, investigating black market adoptions. (324) She was stunned. The blood drained from her face. Clutching the papers, she slammed the door in his face.

"Times a'wasting!" she screamed at the three very pregnant girls, who were setting the table for supper. Throwing her arms in the air, she kicked the back of a chair with her foot.

"What's the matter with you? Can't you ever be on time? You're all a bunch of whores. I've got to figure this out!" she shrieked. The girls rolled their eyes, not daring to look at one another. They had no idea what started the tirade.

Stomping back and forth between the table and the telephone, she swore under her breath.

She threw the papers on the table, as if they burned her fingers.

She couldn't go to Chicago! She couldn't let that happen! This called for desperate measures!

It was too late for her to call the attorney at his office. She shuffled through a stack of papers, looking for his home phone number.

Finding the number, she shouted to the girls. "Be quiet while I'm on the phone!"

Her fingers shaking, she dialed the number on the rotary phone. Attorney W. Custer Service wasn't answering. She slammed down the phone.

Next she called O. B. Martin who had been her attorney when she first opened the maternity home. He wasn't surprised by the call. He knew she had been interviewed. He told her she could not be forced to testify. "Just get your doctor to write a note that you're sick," he told her.

She breathed a sigh of relief. "Is that all I have to do? Dr. Catto should have no problem writing a note. Hell's bells, he owes me. I've taken enough pregnant girls off his hands!" she exclaimed.

As soon as Mae learned the note was in the mail, she dismissed Kefauver from her mind. Chicago was a long way off. She needed to concentrate on problems that were close to home. Nothing much had ever come of the mutterings of politicians, anyway, she reasoned. She refused to be upset by the uproar unless she had to be. Ruby Hightower, a maternity home operator from Texarkana, Texas, had out-maneuvered them, and she could, too!

"There are more births in the State of Oklahoma than taxpayers can take care of. Childless couples will always need me," she told herself.

She had a large household to run. The phone kept ringing. Prospective adoptive parents called continually to ask questions. Birth mothers had to be kept in line to "do the right thing." Their parents needed a listening ear. Mae Marshall tried to be all things to all people. In her mind, she could change the world one baby at a time—regardless of anyone else's opinion.

The basic charge of one hundred dollars per month per birth mother in the 1950s allowed her to believe anything was possible—if she desired it badly enough. (325)

After enjoying local celebrity status as the maternity home madam, Mae had no clue what a national media spotlight could do to bring the winds of change down the plains from Chicago to Edmond and the State of Oklahoma.

As calm as any house could be with two teenaged girls, plus six to eight pregnant women, Mae Marshall's home life rocked along in the summer of 1955. She was sure nothing would come of the hearing in Chicago. State law always trumped federal law when it came to births and families. She had not broken any laws.

The first local media publicity was short and to the point. An Associated Press story in *The Daily Oklahoman* reported Estes Kefauver believed infants were being placed for quick adoption in an apparent racket that stretched across the United States. A Canadian carnival worker who was bringing babies into the United States from Canada testified that he wasn't smuggling, but "giving the babies good homes." (326) Subcommittee investigator Ernest Mitler said babies were placed for $600–$900, while other testimony reported fees being between $2,100 and $5,000.

The evening of the same day, the *Oklahoma City Times* reported an Oklahoma City couple testified they had adopted a blind baby through Mae Marshall. (327) They said they paid Marshall $675.

A longer article appeared on the front page of *The Daily Oklahoman* on the following day. (328) It reported the sub-committee was only seeking to determine whether a federal law was needed to curb non-agency adoptions.

Mae Marshall's home and the blind baby adopted by an Oklahoma City couple was noted. They said they loved the child and planned to keep him.

Later in the month, a front-page story in the *Edmond Booster* told readers about Kefauver writing a note of thanks to Lee Carson, Edmond's chief of police, and to J. B. Marshall, Edmond's city manager, for their help with the investigation. (329) No known relationship exists between Mae and J. B. Marshall.

Mae breathed a sigh of relief. Everything was going according to plan. Summer gave way to fall. Her girls were back in school. There were always new pregnant moms to shepherd through the system.

Dr. W. B. Catto, who wrote her "sick" note for the committee, was on the staff of El Reno's new Park View Hospital. Although it was forty miles west of Oklahoma City, there was plenty of maternity space and the girls would receive great care. Mae believed Catto was a good doctor. The community hospital opened in 1954.

The first Mae Marshall birth mother was admitted to Parkview on October 25, 1955. The baby was discharged on November 8, 1955. The infant may have had some medical problems, because the bill was double the amount of other newborns. The next Mae Marshall birth at the hospital was stillborn.

There were four more Mae Marshall admissions to Park View Hospital in February, 1956. One birth mother paid her own bill and took the baby. Three sets of adoptive parents picked up their babies from the hospital, paying the entire hospital bill, for both mother and baby. (330)

On February 24, 1956, *Oklahoma City Times* reporter Claire Conley called Robert E. Trimble, Park View's administrator, to ask about its policy regarding maternity cases. She also talked to the chairman of the hospital's Board of Control, Lon C. Booth.

Once alerted, they called a special hospital board meeting for that very evening to discuss the hospital's position with regard to questionable adoption practices. The birth mothers were all patients of W. B. Catto, M.D. (331)

Dr. Catto told board members he was

engaged only to deliver the babies and that he had nothing to do with disposition of the babies when they were discharged from the hospital....I had no contract with Mrs. Marshall...and that it was just another obstetrical case to me and the birth certificates are all in order. (332)

Hospital committee members voted against accepting another patient from any privately sponsored maternity home. And no illegitimate baby would be discharged to anyone but his or her own mother, or the mother's legal guardian.

The headline for Claire Conley's article in the next day's *Oklahoma City Times* read, "Grey Market Upset… State Hospital to Snarl Baby Adoption Deals." (333) Conley wrote she learned of the Marshall/Park View connection when a birth mother complained she was not allowed to see her baby, "because Mrs.

Marshall said so!" (334)

Conley reported the hospital did not require the birth mothers to sign a consent form, giving the adoptive parents the right to take her child from the hospital. The babies who were being adopted by Texas and Louisiana couples were not taken to any Oklahoma court for guardianship or any other legal action.

While Trimble was only 29 years old, he had been an administrator for two other hospitals. He was also a member of the American Hospital Association and secretary of the Oklahoma State Hospital Association.

On February 27, administrators from eight central counties of the Oklahoma State Hospital Association voted to request its parent group recommend stricter adoption laws, so hospitals would not be involved in any gray or black market adoption practices. (335)

The State Hospital Association responded by asking the El Reno Hospital Board of Control to rescind its new policy against releasing illegitimate children to prospective adoptive parents.

Cleveland Rodgers, executive secretary of the hospital association, said that hospitals were caught in the middle. They couldn't enforce laws that don't exist. "Hospitals can't refuse emergencies and women in labor are emergencies." (336) Rodgers and four hospital administrators from across the state attended a Park View Board of Control meeting, where members rescinded their earlier resolution. The administrators praised the operation of Park View Hospital. They found nothing ethically wrong with the way the hospital had handled the births.

Dave Huffman, a Muskogee, Oklahoma, hospital administrator, said "If the births in question had occurred (at his hospital), his action would have been the same as that taken by Robert Trimble, the Park View administrator." (337)

Kenneth Wallace, Tulsa's St. John's Hospital administrator, said the situation would continue "until state laws on adoption and on the operation of homes for unwed mothers are changed." (338)

The publicity pushed the Oklahoma Medical Association, the Oklahoma Hospital Association and various welfare groups to lobby the legislature for laws that would make it more difficult for private maternity homes to place children for adoption.

In 1957, the Oklahoma State Legislature passed two adoption bills. One was to require a social investigation of prospective adoptive couples. The other bill made "trafficking in children" a crime. "Trafficking" was defined as (1) accepting compensation in money, property, or other thing of value from a person adopting a child by any person for services performed in connection with an adoption, excluding medical care and legal fees (2) accepting any compensation by any person from anyone else, in return for assisting to place a child for adoption (3) offering to place a child for adoption as an inducement to any woman to enter any maternity home and (4) bringing or sending a child across state lines for the purpose of adoption, without first obtaining consent from the Department of Human Services. A first offense was a misdemeanor with jail time of one year. A second offense became a felony and the punishment was fixed at two years in the state penitentiary. (339)

Mae Marshall continued to assert that she was only a boarding home for unmarried mothers.

On November 8, 1957, an Indiana birth mother signed a complaint against Marshall, alleging that, on August 29, 1957, she offered "to place her child for adoption as an inducement to…(the birth mother) to enter an institution or home, the Mae Marshall Maternity Home, for maternity care and for the delivery of a child." (340) Marshall was arrested and jailed the same day.

An *Oklahoma City Times* article, titled "Charge Filed in Adoption Racket Probe" reported the Indiana birth mother signed a document for Mrs. Marshall, which said she would pay her own board bill, if she left the facility on her own. (341) District Attorney James W. (Bill) Berry, and his assistant, Robert H. Reynolds, believed Marshall was using adoption as an inducement to enter the maternity home.

Marshall spent the weekend in jail. On Monday, she pleaded not guilty and posted $1,500 bail. Her attorney, O. B. Martin, asked Judge Dwain D. Box to find the new law against trafficking in children to be unconstitutional. In the motion to set aside the information contained in the charge, Martin wrote that the law violated Oklahoma's constitution, because the subject was not clearly stated in the title. Judge Box refused to dismiss the complaint.

According to Marshall, nothing was her fault. She blamed her nemesis, Deaconess Hospital, the Home of Redeeming Love, for her troubles. The birth mother who signed the complaint had lived in the Mae Marshall Home for six weeks. Her parents contacted Deaconess about Marshall. A hospital official wrote to the parents, telling them that Marshall's home was a black market establishment and the state was in the process of shutting her down. The birth mother ran away from the Marshall home to enter the Home of Redeeming Love.

Marshall was livid. She filed a lawsuit for libel and slander against Deaconess, asking for $25,000, claiming the statements in the letter were

wholly false and untrue, and such statements were
maliciously made and published by the defendant with
the intent and purpose to blacken and injure the
honesty, virtue, integrity, morality and reputation of the
said plaintiff and her business, and to expose her to
public contempt and ridicule, and to injure and damage
her business. (342)

The maternity home operator also wanted to be compensated
for $600, which was the amount she would have received for the
birth mother's room-and-board for 150 days. She asked for an
injunction to permanently enjoin the defendants from publishing
any future false statements regarding her or her home.

Attorneys negotiated back and forth. The birth mother moved
back to her home state of Indiana. Without a complaining witness,
the case could not go to trial. The Oklahoma County district
attorney dropped the charges on August 20, 1958. Marshall
withdrew her suit against Deaconess Hospital.

The Daily Oklahoman reported Marshall would close her home
east of the college by December 15, 1958. (343) During her career
as a maternity home operator, she said she had arranged for the
adoption of eleven hundred babies of pregnant women, who had
lived at Mae Marshall's Private Home for Unfortunate Girls.

Marshall sold her seven-room home. It was broken up into
apartments for Central State University students. (344)

After spending time with family members, she moved into a
small duplex in Gilmer, Texas. She died in a Gladewater, Texas,
nursing home on February 29, 1976, at the age of 80. Her remains
are buried in the Enon Cemetery, outside of Gilmer, Texas, next to

her baby son.

While there were other maternity homes in Oklahoma, none compared in notoriety with the Mae Marshall Private Home for Unfortunate Girls. Perhaps what made her home unique was Mae's personal flamboyance, coupled with the lax adoption laws, which allowed her to turn a blind eye to the necessity for proper standards and honesty in adoption placement.

Her records have never been found. Persons, who were adopted through the Mae Marshall home and wish to investigate their medical history, are left to scrutinize the original birth certificate for any kernel of truth that may be hiding there. Years can go by while he or she tracks down every lead. Success is not always at the end of the tunnel.

When birth and adoption records were closed, most state legislators were older men who were born in the late 1800s or early 1900s. Their worldview discouraged the rights of children to know their history. First, they didn't believe children would want to know. And second, in their opinion, it wasn't important anyway. They didn't ask any adult adopted persons how they felt about their records. And if the records were sealed, who would know, or care, if untruthful information was placed on the legal documents?

Mae Marshall was gone, but the legacy of fictionalized records lived on.

EPILOGUE

We have uncovered four major secrets in adoption history:

1. North American Indians practiced adoption as a fair and just method of child care, in addition to providing an adult labor force when it was required. Colonists learned about adoption as they patterned their fraternities after the social organization of Indian tribes.

2. The first formalized adoptions were birth fathers adopting their own illegitimate children. Legislators soon gave county judges the task of approving adoption petitions and signing the decrees. It was only a matter of time before judges began to approve the adoption of children by nonrelatives.

3. As more and more children came before the courts as neglected or dependent, state officials had to provide care. When orphanages and reformatories were full, pressure mounted to place children with voluntary social agencies or to place them in private homes. Legislators, worried about their budget, considered any adoptive home to be a wonderful opportunity for a child.

4. Unregulated adoption agencies and individual facilitators proliferated when legislators refused to issue standards and mandate home studies.

The State of Oklahoma was the 46th state to join the United States. Although its residents were late comers to the union, the state is a perfect choice to highlight its adoption history, because of the many Indian tribes who settled there. Every event shaped the next phase of its history. City, county and state governments were charged with the care of children and family units. As the federal government grew larger during the 1930s, bureaucrats pressed for the professionalism of social workers and the confidentiality of records.

Now we are ready for Volume 2, *Adoption's Hidden History: Steps to Sealing the Records*, where we will discover how U. S. Supreme Court justices viewed adoption, how the Children's Bureau began and what happened when federal officials with Social Security pushed for sealing the pre-adoption birth certificates and adoption records in an effort to increase the integrity of state welfare department files.

END NOTES

End Notes for Chapter 1 (Early American Indians)

1. Nancy Bonvillain, *Hiawatha: The Founder of the Iroquois Confederacy* (New York: Chelsea House, 1992). Also Paul Wallace, *White Roots of Peace* (Philadelphia: University of Pennsylvania Press, 1946).
2. _____, *Realm of the Iroquois* (New York: Time-Life Books, 1993), pp. 50–53.
3. Nancy Bonvillain, *The Huron* (New York: Chelsea House Publishers, 1989), pp. 58–59.
4. William N. Fenton, *The Law* and *the Longhouse* (Norman, Oklahoma: University of Oklahoma Press, 1998), p. 32.
5. Richard Slotkin, *Regeneration Through Violence: Mythology of the American Frontier, 1600–1860* (Middletown, Connecticut: Wesleyan University Press, 1973), p. 123.
6. Robert L. Hall, *An Archaeology of the Soul: North American Indian Belief and Ritual* (Urbana, Illinois: University of Illinois Press, 1997), p. 14.
7. *Ibid.*, p. 11.
8. Carl Reser, *Lewis Henry Morgan: American Scholar* (Chicago, Illinois: University of Chicago Press, 1960), p. 27.
9. Lewis Henry Morgan, *League of the Ho-de-no-sau-nee, or Iroquois* (New York: Dodd, Mead and Company, 1922), p. 318.

Reprint.

10. *Ibid.*, p. 326.

11. *Ibid.*, p. 333.

12. *Op.cit*, Reser, p. 71.

13. *Ibid.*, p. 37.

14. Lewis Henry Morgan, *Ancient Society, or Researches in the Lines of Human Progress from Savagery through Barbarism to Civilization* (New Brunswick, New Jersey: Transaction Publications, 2000). Originally published in Calcutta: Bharatti Library, 1877. On page 81, Morgan gives a brief description of an adoption ceremony:

"After the people had assembled at the council house, one of the chiefs made an address giving some account of the person(the adoptee), the reason for his adoption, the name of the gens of the person adopting, and the name bestowed on the novitiate. Two chiefs taking the person by the arms then marched with him through the council house and back, chanting the song of adoption...."

15. Printed with permission from the Department of Rare Books and Special Collections, University of Rochester Library, Unpublished manuscript, "Initiation Ceremony," Lewis Henry Morgan papers, Box 21, Folder 19.

16. *Ibid.*

17. *Ibid.*

18. *Ibid.*

19. *Ibid.*

20. *Ibid.*

21. Roger A. Bruns, *John Wesley Powell: Explorer of the Grand Canyon* (Springfield, New Jersey: Enslow Publications, Inc., 1997), p. 57.

22. *Ibid*, p. 100.

23. Joan Mark, *A Stranger in Her Native Land* (Lincoln, Nebraska: University of Nebraska Press, 1988), p. 207.

24. Alice Cunningham Fletcher and Francis LaFlesche, *The Omaha Tribe*, Part 1 (Washington, D.C.: Government Printing Office, 1911), pp. 61–62. [Originally published as the 27th

Annual Report of the Bureau of American Ethnology to the Secretary of the Smithsonian Institution, 1905–06].

25. Alice C. Fletcher, *The Hako: A Pawnee Ceremony*, Second Annual Report, Part 2 of the Bureau of American Ethnology (Washington, D.C.: U. S. Government Printing Office, 1904), p. 17.

26. *Ibid.*, p. 148.

27. *Ibid.*, p. 13.

End Notes for Chapter 2 (Tales of Indian Captivities)

28. Richard Slotkin, *Regeneration Through Violence: Mythology of the American Frontier, 1600–1860* (Middletown, Connecticut: Wesleyan University Press, 1973), p. 268.

29. Matthew Brayton, *The Indian Captive* (Fostoria, Ohio: Gray Printing Co., 1896).

30. See also Larry Hancks, "The Emigrant Tribes: Wyandot, Delaware and Shawnee–A Chronology," n.d., (http://www.cc.ukans.edu/kansas/wn/emigrant.htm, accessed August 9, 2001).

31. The gauntlet is a form of torture in which the captive is forced to run between two lines of Indians. Each warrior pummels the slave with a club or other weapon.

32. William E. Connelley (ed.), *The Provisional Government of Nebraska Territory and the Journals of William Walker* (Lincoln, Nebraska: Nebraska Historical Society, 1899), p. 7. Reprinted privately in 1996 by Rose Stauber, Grove, Oklahoma.

33. *Ibid.*, n. 4, p. 3.

34. James T. DeShields, *Border Wars of Texas* (Tioga, Texas: The Herald Company, 1912).

35. J. Norman Heard, *White Into Red* (Metuchen, New Jersey: The Scarecrow Press, Inc., 1973).

36. M. K. Wisehart, *Sam Houston: American Giant* (Washington, D.C.: Robert B. Luce, Inc., 1962), p. 10.

37. Temple Houston, unpublished manuscript, Oklahoma Historical Society vertical file, Oklahoma City, Oklahoma.

38. Unpublished manuscript, "Ela-Teecha," Pauls Valley Public Library vertical file, Pauls Valley, Oklahoma.
39. Bill Paul and Cindy Paul, *Shadow of an Indian Star* (Austin, Texas: Synergy Books, 2005).
40. _____, "Sousa Made Ponca Chief," *Newkirk Herald Journal* (October 18, 1928), p. 1.
41. _____, "Osage Tribal Council Confirms Adoption of Bishop into Tribe," *Southwest Courier* (April 22, 1950), p. 1.

End Notes for Chapter 3 (Fraternities)

42. Robert E. Davis, *History of the Improved Order of Red Men and the Degree of Pocahontas* (Waco, Texas: Davis Brothers Publishing Company, Inc., 1990), p. 17.
43. The Gordian Knot was a Greek myth. The knot was a rope jumbled up in a tight coil, with no ends showing. It was said that the person who could untie the rope and solve the puzzle would conquer all of Asia.
44. Elizabeth Tooker, *Lewis H. Morgan on Iroquois Material Culture* (Tucson, Arizona: University of Arizona Press, 1994), p. 17.
45. *Op.cit.*, Davis, pp. 360–1.
46. *Ibid.,* p. 418-9. Governors Flem D. Sampson of Kentucky and John H. Trumbull of Connecticut were also adopted in 1930.
47. *Ibid.*, pp. 100–101.
48. See (<http://www.redmen.org>, accessed 2/11/03).
49. _____, "Red Men of State will Arrive in City Today to Attend Annual Council Meetings to be Held in State House Tuesday," *Illinois State Journal* (October 5, 1919), p. 2.
50. _____, "Pocahontas to Meet," *Illinois State Journal* (October 5, 1919), p. 2.
51. Joseph Samuel Murrow and William Moses Anderson, *Murrow Masonic Monitor* (Oklahoma: The Grand Lodge A.F. & A.M., 1920), p. 31. Murrow was a mason and a missionary to the Choctaw Indians in Oklahoma.
52. *Ibid.*, p. 84.

53. Albert Pike, *Masonry of Adoption: Masonic Rituals for Women* (Montana: Kessinger Publishing, 1992), p. 18. Reprint from 1866.

54. *Ibid.*, p. 34.

55. *Ibid.*, p. 92.

56. The term "melioristic" sounds derogatory, but it means that his social theories were to improve society.

57. Alvin F. Nelson, *The Development of Lester Ward's World View* (Fort Worth, Texas: Branch System, Inc., 1968), p. 19.

58. Samuel Chugerman, *Lester F. Ward: The American Aristotle* (Durham, North Carolina: Duke University Press, 1939), p. 59.

59. *Ibid.*, p. 167.

60. Donald Worster, *The River Running West* (New York: Oxford University Press, 2001), p. 447.

End Notes for Chapter 4 (The Orphan Train)

61. Matthew A. Crenshaw, *Building the Invisible Orphanage* (Cambridge, Massachusetts: Harvard University Press, 1998), p. 63.

62. _____, "To the Public—Children's Aid Society," *New York Daily Times* (March 2, 1853), p. 8.

63. _____, "The Children's Aid Society," *New York Herald* (February 22, 1874), p. 7.

64. Brace's views were taken from a collection of letters, with anecdotal biography, written and edited by Emma Brace. See Emma Brace (ed.), *The Life of Charles Loring Brace* (New York: Charles Scriber, 1894). Reprint edition (New York: Arno Press, 1976).

65. Coy F. Cross, *Go West, Young Man! Horace Greeley's Vision For America* (Albuquerque, New Mexico: University of New Mexico Press, 1995), p. 7. In the early 1840s, Greeley began to encourage poor readers of New York City's *Weekly Tribune* to migrate west for lucrative opportunities in agriculture.

66. Dorothy Zietz, *Child Welfare: Principle and Methods* (New York: Wiley, 1959), p. 60; the words "implanted by Christianity" are quoted from "The 'Placing Out' Plan for the

Homeless and Vagrant Children" in *Proceedings of the Conference of Charities* (Albany, New York: John Munsell, 1876), pp. 139–144.

67. *Ibid.*, p. 201.
68. Charles Loring Brace, "Walks Among the New York Poor," *New York Daily Times* (October 11, 1852), p. 1. Mr. Pease was probably Louis M. Pease, who was the first director of the Five Points Mission, which was established by the Ladies' Methodist Home Missionary Society. See Stephen O'Connor, *Orphan Trains: The Story of Charles Loring Brace and the Children He Saved and Failed* (New York: Houghton Mifflin Company, 2001), p. 73.
69. Charles Loring Brace, *The Dangerous Classes of New York and Twenty Years' Work Among Them* (New York: Wynkoop and Hallenbeck, 1880; reprinted edition (Montclair, New Jersey: Patterson Smith, 1967), p. 14.
70. H. Addington Bruce, "The Boy Who Goes Wrong," *The Century Magazine*, Vol. 87, Number 4 (February, 1914), pp. 542–546.

End Notes for Chapter 5 (The New Abolitionists)

71. _____, "Partners: How Social Hygiene Works With You in Your Community to Build Healthy Personal and Family Life," *Journal of Social Hygiene*, Vol. 36, Number 8 (November, 1958), p. 340
72. David J. Pivar, *Purity Crusade: Sexual Morality and Social Control, 1868-1900* (Westport, Connecticut: Greenwood Press, Inc., 1973), p. 7.
73. Sarah Hopper Emerson (*ed.*), *The Life of Abby Hopper Gibbons* (New York: G.P. Putnam's, 1896).
74. Mrs. E. S. Turner, "An Equal Standard of Morals—Some Plain Words on a Forbidden Subject," *The Philanthropist*, Vol. IX, No. 5 (May, 1894), p. 1.
75. *Ibid.*
76. *Ibid.*
77. Aaron M. Powell, *The National Purity Congress, Its Papers,*

Addresses, Portraits (New York: The American Purity Alliance, 1896), p. 302. Reprinted in New York by Arno Press, 1976.

78. *Ibid.*, p. 182

79. _____, "Only a Working Girl," *Justice*, April 19, 1907, p. 1.

80. _____, "White Slaves," *Justice*, May 31, 1907, p. 1.

81. Mammon is something considered evil, sinful or greedy.

82. John Walter Sams, "White Slaves of America," *Justice*, January 11, 1907, p. 1.

83. _____, "Plenty of Homes for Baby Boy," *Daily Oklahoman* (October 18, 1910), p. 4 and _____, "Aid Has a Little Girl for Adoption," *Daily Oklahoman* (October 24, 1910), p. 7.

84. _____, "The State Bills," *Vigilance*, Vol. XXIII, No. 7 (April, 1910), p. 9.

85. Jessie Hodder, "Helping the Unfortunate," *Vigilance*, Vol. XXIII, No. 7 (April 1910), p. 16. History of Women Series, Reel 172.

86. David Starr Jordan, "Like the Seed is the Harvest," *Vigilance*, Vol. XXV, No. 6 (June, 1912), p. 2.

87. _____, "Study of Illegitimacy, " *Vigilance*, Vol. XXV, No. 8 (August, 1912), p. 32.

88. _____, "The Myth of the Educated Prostitute," *Vigilance*, Vol. XXVII, No. 12 (December, 1913), p. 2.

89. S. W. Dickinson, "Correspondence: Illegitimacy," *Vigilance*, Vol. XXVI, Number 1 (January, 1913), p. 29.

90. Benjamin R. Andrews, "Anna Garlin Spencer and Education for the Family," *Journal of Social Hygiene*, Vol. XVIII, No. 4 (April,1932), p. 186.

91. _____, "Abstracts of Periodical Literature," *Social Hygiene*, Vol. 7, No. 1 (January, 1921), p. 109.

92. _____, "The Unmarried Mother," *The Social Hygiene Bulletin*, Vol. IX, No. 5 (May, 1922), p. 4.

93. William J. Gibbons, "Religion as a Force for Sex Morality," *Journal of Social Hygiene*, Vol. 36, No. 4 (April, 1950), p. 140.

End Notes for Chapter 6 (Chicago Child Saving)

94. _____, "Chinese Child Lost," *Chicago Evening Journal* (May 4, 1898), p. 6. (http://gale.cengage.com, available to subscrib-ing institutions, accessed 7-26-2010)

95. _____, "A Brief Recount of History Surrounding the Children's Home & Aid Society Du Quoin Receiving Home," (http://www.perrycountyillinois.net/sub424.htm, accessed 1-12-09).

96. LeRoy Ashby, *Saving the Waifs: Reformers and Dependent Children, 1890–1917* (Philadelphia, Pennsylvania: Temple University Press, 1984), p. 41.

97. *Ibid.*, p. 44.

98. _____. "Biographical Sketch," University of Illinois at Chicago, Special Collections, (http://www.uic.edu/depts/lib/specialcoll/services/rjd/finding aids/Jlathropf.html, accessed 1-10-2009). Lathrop became the first director of the U. S. Children's Bureau. Although she was from a well-to-do family, Lathrop spent her whole life trying to better the lives of children. The seed of her enthusiasm for children may have germinated when she acted the part of a "slavey," shining shoes in a school play. "Slavey" was a term used to denote dependent children, who had to work to put food on the family's table, or at the very least, to support themselves. See Jane Addams, *My Friend, Julia Lathrop* (Chicago: University of Chicago Press, 2004), p. 27.

99. Timothy D. Hurley, *Origin of the Illinois Juvenile Court Law* (Chicago, Illinois: The Visitation and Aid Society, 1907), p. 18.

100. *Ibid.*

101. For an in-depth perspective on Judge Tuthill and the juvenile court, see (http://www.futureofchildren.org/usr_doc/vol6no3ART2/pdf, accessed 1-19-2009). Reprinted from Sanford J. Fox, "The Early History of the Court," *The Juvenile Court*, Vol. 6, Number 3 (Winter 1996), pp. 29–39.

102. *Op.cit.*, Hurley, p. 17.
103. Portions of the *Juvenile Court Record* have been placed online by the University of Michigan and the Hathi Trust Library. See REF: (http://mirlyn.lib.umich.edu/F/6E4FK7VIMNL9X6FFLN3F2 BU2EDJ7TC6BPQ3KTYQ7KTYQK4Q6GJD44-64370?func=item-global&doc_library=MIU01&doc_number=000531841&year =&volume=&sub_library=).
104. Hastings H. Hart, "Annual Dinner," *Juvenile Court Record*, Vol. V, Number 1 (January, 1904), p. 12. Hart was a nationally known child welfare worker, who became superintendent of the National Home Society, after Van Arsdale passed away.
105. _____, "What the Juvenile Court Has Accomplished," *Juvenile Court Record*, Vol. V, Number 1 (January 1904), p. 8.
106. Sherman C. Kingsley, "Foundation Principles of Good Child Saving Work," *Juvenile Court Record*, Vol. V, Number 11 (December, 1904), pp. 9–11.
107. *Op.cit.*, Ashby, p. 61.
108. *Ibid.*, p. 67. From the Annual Report of the Superintendent, in Minutes, April 15, 1909.
109. Connie Saint Clare, "Margaret Slocum Sage," (http://learningtogive.org/papers/paper211.html (accessed 1-27-2009). See also (http://www.russellsage.org and http://www.1911encyclopedia.org/Russell_Sage).
110. John Mark Glenn, Lillian Brandt and Frank E. Andrews, *The Russell Sage Foundation—Social Research and Social Action in America, 1907-1947* (New York: Russell Sage Foundation, 1947), p. 60.
111. *Ibid.*, p. 102–3.
112. William H. Slingerland, *Child-Placing in Families: A Manual for Students and Social Workers* (New York: Russell Sage Foundation, 1919).
113. Ellen Herman, *Kinship By Design* (Chicago, Illinois: University of Chicago Press, 2008).

114. _____, "Selection of Homes," *Juvenile Court Record*, Vol. VI, Number 2 (February 1905), p. 13.

End Notes for Chapter 7 (Adoption's Legal Basis)

115. Microfiche–*Session Laws of Tennessee*, 1801, Chapter 42 (Westport, Connecticut: Redgrave Information Resources, Inc.), p. 317.

116. Microfiche–*Session Laws of Tennessee*, 1803, Chapters 36, 41 and 50 (Westport, Connecticut: Redgrave Information Resources, Inc.), pp. 38–39, 82–83, 94–95.

117. Microfiche–*Session Laws of Tennessee*, 1805, Chapter 2 (Westport, Connecticut: Redgrave Information Resources, Inc.), p. 4.

118. Microfiche–*Session Laws of Tennessee*, 1805, Chapter 3 (Westport, Connecticut: Redgrave Information Resources, Inc.), p. 4–5

119. Microfiche–*Session Laws of Tennessee*, 1852, Chapter 2 (Westport, Connecticut: Redgrave Information Resources, Inc.), p. 618

120. Microfiche–*Session Laws of Kentucky*, 1841, Chapter 84 (Westport, Connecticut: Redgrave Information Resources, Inc.), p. 132.

121. Microfiche–*General Laws of Texas*, Third Legislature, 1849 (Westport, Connecticut: Redgrave Information Resources, Inc.), p. 136.

122. _____, "Deeds Ownership of Boy," *New York Times*, October 15, 1921, p. 14.

123. Emelyn F. Peck, *Adoption Laws in the United States* (Washington, D.C.: U. S. Government Printing Office, 1925), p. 3. [Children's Bureau Publication #148]

124. Peck footnotes Michigan and Montana, specifically.

125. *Ibid.*

126. Microfiche–*Session Laws of Massachusetts*, 1851, Chapter 32 (Westport, Connecticut: Redgrave Information Resources, Inc.), pp. 815–816.

127. Microfiche–*Session Laws of Illinois*, 1867, "Minors," (Westport, Connecticut: Redgrave Information Resources, Inc.), pp. 133-134.
128. Microfiche–*Session Laws of New York*, 1873, Chapter 830 (Westport, Connecticut: Redgrave Information Resources, Inc.), pp. 1243–1245.
129. Microfiche–*Session Laws of Minnesota*, 1917, Chapter 397 (Westport, Connecticut: Redgrave Information Resources, Inc.), p. 335.
130. *Ibid.*, p. 337.
131. Microfiche–*Oklahoma's Organic Act of 1890* (Westport, Connecticut: Redgrave Information Resources, Inc.), p. 13.
132. Microfiche–*Territorial Laws of Oklahoma*, 1895, Chapter 17 (Westport, Connecticut: Redgrave Information Resources, Inc.), p. 179. "Collateral kindred" are adoptive aunts, uncles, grandparents and siblings. Some adopted children were barred from inheriting from their adoptive parents because judges did not recognize the petition and decree as binding for inheritance. They did not have a birth certificate that certified the relationship with their adoptive parents.
133. Microfiche–*Territorial Laws of Oklahoma*, 1905, Chapter 14 (Westport, Connecticut: Redgrave Information Resources, Inc.), p. 204.
134. *Ibid.*, p. 208.
135. Microfiche–*Session Laws of Oklahoma*, 1907–08 (Westport, Connecticut: Redgrave Information Resources, Inc.), p. 269.
136. *Ibid.*, p. 270.
137. Microfiche–*Session Laws of Oklahoma*, 1915, Chapter 145 (Xerox University Microfilms, Ann Arbor, Michigan), p. 191.

End Notes for Chapter 8 (Oklahoma Pioneers)

138. Mary Hewett Bailey, *A History of Grady County, Oklahoma*, a thesis in partial fulfillment of the requirements for Master of Arts (Norman, Oklahoma: University of Oklahoma, 1937), p. 37.

139. William H. Murray, *Memories of Governor Murray and the True History of Oklahoma*, Vol. 1 (Boston: Meador Publishing Co., 1945), p. 36.
140. Pamela Prigmore, *The Murray Administration*, a thesis in partial fulfillment of the requirements for Master of Arts (Norman, Oklahoma: University of Oklahoma, 1948), p. 7-8.
141. *Op.cit.*, Murray, p. 207-8.
142. _____, *The Constitution of Oklahoma* (Guthrie: Leader Printing Company, 1907), p. 19. Oklahoma State Archives.
143. Oklahoma's Constitution is on-line. The address is (<http://oklegal.onenet.netokcon/V-46.html>, accessed September 6, 2011).
144. Oscar Presley Fowler, *The Haskell Regime* (Oklahoma City: Boles Printing Company, Inc., 1933), p. 17.
145. *Ibid.*, p. 21.
146. Kate Barnard, Oklahoma Historical Society's Vertical File, Oklahoma City, Oklahoma.
147. Edith Copeland, "Miss Kate of Oklahoma," University of Oklahoma Western History Collection, Copeland Collection, Box 4, FF1.
148. Bob Burke and Glenda Carlile, *Kate Barnard: Oklahoma's Good Angel* (Edmond, Oklahoma: University of Central Oklahoma Press, 2001), p. 15.
149. *Op.cit.*, Copeland Collection, Box 1, FF 7, p. 48.
150. Families, who could prove the child's income was needed for support, were given a stipend to replace the lost wages while the children were in school. This applied to teenagers, 14–16 years old, who were unaffected by the Child Labor Law.
151. *Op.cit.*, Copeland Collection, Letter replying to Theodore Dreiser, November 28, 1908, Box 1, FF 8.
152. *Op.cit.*, Burke and Carlile, p. 55.
153. _____, "Rules of Procedure in Probate Matters Adopted by the County Judges of the Five Civilized Tribes Portion of Oklahoma," 63rd Congress, 2d Session, House of Representatives, Document No. 758.

End Notes for Chapter 9 (Dumpster Babies)

154. _____, "Lifeless Body Found in Box," *The Daily Oklahoman* (March 5, 1911), p. 16.
155. _____, "Sentenced to Hang," *Vinita Indian Chieftain* (May 26, 1887), p. 3.
156. _____, untitled, *El Reno News* (October 16, 1896), p. 2.
157. _____, "Charged with Killing Own Child: Mr. and Mrs. (Smith) Arrested for Heinous Crime," *The Stratford Tribune* (February 10, 1911), p. 1.
158. _____, "(Smith) Found Not Guilty," *Pauls Valley Enterprise* (February 23, 1911), p. 1.
159. _____, "Mother Murders Babe by Choking," *Sayre Searchlight* (August 19, 1909), p. 1.
160. _____, "Infanticide," *Elk City Democrat-Statesman* (August 19, 1909), p. 1.
161. _____, "District Court Proceedings," *Sayre Searchlight* (March 18, 1910), p. 8.
162. Lionel Rose, *Massacre of Innocents: Infanticide in Britain 1800-1939* (London: Routledge & Kegan, 1986), p. 3.
163. *Ibid.*, p. 38.
164. Mary Boyle O'Reilly, "The Daughters of Herod," *New England Magazine*, Vol. XLIII (November, 1910), p. 279.
165. *Ibid.*, p. 282.
166. *Ibid.*, p. 286.
167. _____, "Baby Farmer is Going to Move," *The Daily Oklahoman* (September 14, 1907), p. 4.
168. _____, "Body of Infant Discovered by Boys," *The Daily Oklahoman* (March 18, 1908), p. 12.
169. _____, "Baby Traffic Disgraceful Says Strubble," *The Daily Oklahoman* (April 14, 1908), p. 12.
170. It is unclear whether this particular Bethany Hospital was located in the City of Bethany or elsewhere.
171. _____, "Baby Farms to be Inspected in 10 Days," *The Daily Oklahoman* (May 23, 1908), p. 6.
172. _____, "Exposure Cause of Baby's Death," *The Daily Oklahoman* (October 8, 1907), p. 2.
173. _____, "Baby Deserted by its Mother," *The Daily*

Oklahoman (October 4, 1907), p. 7.

174. ____, "Will Adopt Baby Boy Left by Child Wife," *The Daily Oklahoma*n (December 8, 1907), p. 14.

175. ____, "Babies will be in One Keeping," *The Daily Oklahoman* (February 18, 1908), p. 5.

176. ____, "Nameless Tot Kidnapped by its Foster Mother," *The Daily Oklahoman* (August 26, 1908), p. 1.

177. ____, "Foster Mother Must Give Babe Away in Court Today," *The Daily Oklahoman* (August 29, 1908), p. 1.

178. ____, "Will Battle in Court for Unfortunate Babe," *The Daily Oklahoman* (August 27, 1908), p. 1.

179. Mattie Cal Gibson, *The Dependent Family in the Oklahoma City Community Camp*, a thesis in partial fulfillment of the requirements for Master of Arts (Norman, Oklahoma: University of Oklahoma, 1934), p. 2.

180. Mary Grace Lee, *The Disposition of Orphans*, a thesis in partial fulfillment of the requirements for Master of Arts (Norman, Oklahoma: University of Oklahoma, 1911), p. 15.

181. *Ibid.*, p. 16.

182. ____, "Whitaker Home at Pryor Builds Fine Record," *Muskogee Daily Phoenix* (March 14, 1897), p. 5.

183. Seth K. Corden and W. B. Richards (ed.), *Oklahoma Red Book, Vol. II* (Oklahoma City, Oklahoma, 1912), p. 1.

184. ____, "(Jill) Found Guilty After Dramatic Trial," *State Sentinel* (December 9, 1915), p. 1. Pseudonyms are used for the victim and the defendant.

185. Letter from W. D. Matthews, February 18, 1916, stored at the Oklahoma State Archives, Oklahoma City.

186. Epworth School of Medicine merged with the University of Oklahoma School of Medicine. Epworth University became Oklahoma City University, a Methodist college in Oklahoma City.

187. Letter from Mabel Bassett to Dr. C. Curtis Allen, Oklahoma State Archives, RG 36, Series 1, Box 19, FF 22.

188. T. P. Tripp, "Humanitarian Work is Approved in Oklahoma," *Harlow's Weekly*, Vol. 51, #3 (January 20, 1940), pp. 9-10.

189. J. C. Bass, "He Has Brought Up 1,400 Babies and Found

Homes for Them All!" *The Daily Oklahoman* (August 4, 1935), p. C6.
190. *Op.cit.*, Richards, p. 223
191. ____, "Five Children from County in Home," *Wynnewood New Era* (October 2, 1911), p. 1.
192. W. D. Mathews to M. E. Harris, January 24, 1913, Charities and Corrections Collection records, RG 36–1, Box 1, Folder 27, Oklahoma State Archives, Oklahoma City, Oklahoma.
193. *Ibid.*, p. 5.
194. *Ibid.*, p. 6-7.
195. Personal Interview, Diane McCornack, July 27, 2000.
196. Opal Bennefield Clark, *A Fool's Enterprise* (Sand Springs, Oklahoma: Dexter Publishing Company, 1992), p. 84.
197. *Ibid.*, p. 196.

End Notes for Chapter 10 (Rescue Homes)

198. Rev. J. D. Schollenberger, president of the Wichita Rescue Home and pastor of the Free Methodist Church, Wichita Kansas.
199. ____, "Birthday Anniversary," *Albuquerque Journal*, May 23, 1939, p. 3. In addition to Free Methodist rescue missions in Omaha, Guthrie and Enid, Newberry and Dougherty also created rescue missions in Albuquerque, St. Louis, San Antonio and Detroit.
200. Helen Freudenberger Holmes, *Logan County History*, Vol. II (Guthrie, Oklahoma: Logan County Extension Homemakers Council and the Logan County Historical Society, 1980), p. 282.
201. ____, "Residence for a Rescue Home," *Oklahoma State Capitol* (April 3, 1901), p. 5.
202. ____, "Rescue Home Annual Report," *Oklahoma State Capitol* (January 11, 1902), p. 6.
203. *Wichita City Directory*, 1900.
204. George Eliot, *Adam Bede* (New York: Dodd, Mead & Co., 1947), reprinted from the original published in 1859.
205. ____, "Whose Babe Is It?" *The Daily Oklahoman*

(December 30, 1900), p. 1; and "Rescue the Fallen," *Oklahoma State Capitol* (December 30, 1900), p. 4.

206. Article XII of the Free Methodist Church's Constitution defines "adoption:" "Adoption is a filial term full of warmth, love, and acceptance. It denotes that by our new relationship in Christ we have become His wanted children freed from the mastery of both sin and Satan. The believer has the witness of the Spirit that he is a child of God." In the succeeding commentary, author Loyd H. Knox tells church members that adoption is a wonderful metaphor. "Were you an orphan?" he asks. "Now you are God's wanted child!" From "We Believe—Article XII Salvation—The New Life in Christ," *Light and Life*, Vol. 108, Number 12 (July 22, 1975), p. 9.

207. Emma M. Whittemore, *Delia: the Blue-Bird of Mulberry Street* (New York: Fleming H. Revell, 1893).

208. Grass widows were divorced or single women with minor children. They were called grass widows, because they did not receive money for housing. Benefits given to them were called 'outdoor relief' or 'grass relief.'

209. Richard Artemus Lee, *Mother Lee's Experience in Fifteen Years' Rescue Work with Thrilling Incidents of Her Life* (Omaha, Nebraska: privately printed, 1906), p. 256-7.

210. *Ibid.*, p. 284.

211. _____, "May Consolidate Homes for Girls," *The Daily Oklahoman* (March 24, 1909), p. 10.

212. _____, "Rescue Home Project is Given Indorsement," *The Daily Oklahoman* (April 4, 1909), p. 6.

213. _____"The Holmes' Home of Redeeming Love for Erring and Betrayed Girls," *The Daily Oklahoman* (March 31, 1911), p. 6.

214. Allen's obituary in *The Daily Oklahoman* on January 1, 1939, said he was the director of the Rio Grande Home of Redeeming Love in Albuquerque, New Mexico. His sister, Mrs. Newberry, was superintendent of the same home.

215. _____, "These Two Young Men Will Stick Together," *The Daily Oklahoman* (April 10, 1933), p. 1.

216. _____, "Babies Look to Community Fund, Too," *The Daily*

Oklahoman (November 3, 1935), p. A9.

217. _____, "Home Cares for 246 Girls in One Year," *The Daily Oklahoman* (January 24, 1938), p. 9.

218. Charles V. Fairbairn, "Our Charitable Institutions," *The Free Methodist* (September 4, 1942), p. 5.

219. _____, "The Rescue Work is to Continue; Committee on Reorganization Busy with Plans for Future of the Home," *The Daily Oklahoman* (August 8, 1905), p. 5.

220. _____, "Freda Walters Declared Free," *The Daily Oklahoman* (August 17, 1905), p. 2.

221. _____, "Police Matron; Trouble at the Rescue Home," *The Daily Oklahoman* (August 17, 1905), p. 2.

222. _____, "Was Acquitted; Mrs. Bond Fainted when the Court Announced that She was Not Guilty," *The Daily Oklahoman* (August 20, 1905), p. 5.

223. _____, "City Godmother; Cares for Infants," *The Daily Oklahoman* (undated clipping).

224. Leona Bellew McConnell, "A History of the Town and College of Bethany, Oklahoma," thesis in partial fulfillment of the requirements for Master of Arts (Norman, Oklahoma: University of Oklahoma, 1935), p. 1.

225. Emma Irick, *The King's Daughter* (Kansas City, Missouri: Pedestal Press, 1973), p. 40.

226. *Op.cit.*, McConnell, p. 21.

227. "In the Matter of the Nazarene Home: Transcript of Evidence," Oklahoma State Archives, Oklahoma City, Oklahoma, Charities and Corrections Collection records, RG 36–2–3, Box 26, Folder 2, p. 21.

228. It is assumed she is referring to a notebook. The name and location have been shortened for privacy considerations.

229. *Op.Cit.*, "In the Matter of the Nazarene Home," p. 100.

230. *Ibid.*

231. *Ibid.*

232. J.A. Garvey, "Associated Catholic Charities," *Southwest Courier* (May 18, 1940), p. 8.

End Notes for Chapter 11 (Early-Day Media)

233. _____, "Murdered Babes," San Francisco's *Daily Examiner* (March 3, 1887), p. 1; "Hapless Babes," *Daily Examiner* (March 4, 1887), p.1; "Dead Babes," *Daily Examiner* (March 5, 1887), p. 1.

234. _____, "Dead Babes," *Daily Examiner* (March 5, 1887), p. 1.

235. Gerald J. Baldasty, *E. W. Scripps and the Business of Newspapers* (Urbana, Illinois: University of Illinois Press, 1999), p. 15.

236. *Ibid.*, p. 56.

237. _____, "Only Parents Illegitimate," *Oklahoma News* (August 2, 1930), p. 1.

238. Mr. Fixit, "Many Seek to Adopt Babies," *Oklahoma News* (April 13, 1929), p. 11. Mr. Fixit listed the following agencies to which prospective adoptive couples might apply for a child: West Oklahoma Home in Helena, Whittaker State Home in Pryor, Tipton Home in Tipton, St. Joseph's Orphanage and the Baptist Orphanage, both in Oklahoma City, the Methodist Home in Britton, Francis E. Willard Home in Tulsa, and the Sand Springs Home in Sand Springs.

239. _____, "Here's Happiness---! A Happy Boy, Ready to Make a Home of Someone's House, Asks Aid of Mr. Fixit," *Oklahoma News* (March 19, 1929), p. 1.

240. _____, "'Baby Doe' Finds Home: Forsaken 5-Month-Old Boy Brings Cheer to Childless Couple; New Life of Love and Care Is Offered by Wewoka Attorney," *Oklahoma News* (March 25, 1929), p. 1.

241. LeRoy Plumley, "Mr. Fixit Tells of Saving 30 Lives, Finding Homes for 10 Babies During Experience," *Oklahoma News* (August 13, 1933), p. 1.

242. _____, "Police Seek Mother of Two Months Old Girl Abandoned in City Roominghouse," *Oklahoma News* (January 7, 1930), p. 1.

243. _____, "Abandoned 'Label' Baby to Get Good Home," *Oklahoma News* (January 10, 1930), p. 1.

244. *Ibid.*

245. ____,"Label Baby to Get Home, City Judge Decrees," *Oklahoma News* (January 14, 1930), p. 1.

246. ____, "Baby Custody Quiz Delayed," *Oklahoma News* (January 11, 1930), p. 1.

247. ____, "Mother Asks to Recover 'Label' Baby," *Oklahoma News* (January 23, 1930), p. 1-2.

248. ____, "Baby Custody Quiz Delayed," *Oklahoma News* (January 11, 1930), p. 1.

249. ____, "Abandoned 'Baby Maxine,' Girl Mother United Here," *Oklahoma News* (March 10, 1930), p. 2.

250. ____, "Unchaste Woman Makes the Best Mother, States City Judge from Bench," *Oklahoma News* (October 16, 1932), p. 6.

251. ____, "Economic Distress Has No Effect on Baby Adoptions," unidentified and undated clipping.

252. Noel Houston, "Mother Sought for Unborn Baby," *Oklahoma News* (August 20, 1930), p. 1

253. *Ibid.*

254. Mr. Fixit, "Baby May Go to Rich Home," *Oklahoma News* (August 25, 1930), p. 8.

255. Lorren L. Williams, "Girl Mother Asks Mr. Fixit to Find Home for Unborn Baby," *Oklahoma News*, July 7, 1935, p. 1.

256. Irvin S. Cobb, "A Rich Woman's Charities," *Saturday Evening* Post (April 10, 1920), p. 77.

257. C. V. Williams, "Before You Adopt a Child," *Hygeia*, Vol. 2, No. 7 (July 1924), p. 427.

258. Virginia Reid, "Black Market Babies," *Woman's Home Companion*, Vol. 71, No. 12 (December 1944), p. 30.

259. *Ibid.*, p. 31.

260. See *Adoption's Hidden History, Vol. 2*, Chapter 2. "U. S. Supreme Court."

End Notes for Chapter 12 (Oklahoma in the 1930s)

261. Viola Coates Lohmann, *Social Work Resources in Oklahoma*, thesis in partial fulfillment for Master of Arts (Norman, Oklahoma: University of Oklahoma, 1938), p. 25.

262. Ellworth Collings, *The 101 Ranch* (Norman, Oklahoma: University of Oklahoma Press, 1937), p. 104.

263. Glenda Carlile, *Petticoats, Politics, and Pirouettes* (Oklahoma City, Oklahoma: Southern Hills Publishing Company, 1995), p. 51.

264. *Ibid.*, p. 12

265. Patti Apman, *Lyde Roberts Marland: The Princess of the 'Palace on the Prairie,'* (Ponca City, Oklahoma: Marland Estate, 1995), p. 13.

266. Mary Boley, "A Little Girl with a Doll Starts Campaign for Change in Law," *Lawton Morning Press* (June 4, 1944), p. 3.

267. _____, "Doctors Accused of Selling Babies," *Oklahoma City Times* (August 19, 1933), p. 1.

268. _____, "Oklahoma Babies Sold For Adoption," *New York Times* (August 20, 1933), p. 13.

269. _____, "Warnings Issued in 'Baby Market,' *Tulsa World* (August 19, 1933), p. 1.

270. *Ibid.*

271. _____, "Mrs. Bassett Finds Weapon to Check 'Sales' of Babies," *Tulsa Tribune* (August 23, 1933), p. 5.

272. _____, "Court Backs Orphan Home," *The Daily Oklahoman* (December 6, 1936), p. 25A.

273. Dovie Montgomery Kull grew up around Pawhuska, Oklahoma, and graduated from the University of Oklahoma's School of Social Work. She married A. E. Kull, a widower, who was the father of a friend in the Chi Omega Sorority. Kull worked as a car salesman and, in the late 1920s, wrote a political column for *Harper's Weekly*, entitled "Kullings." He called Jess Harper, the "best legislator in the state." Harper later became head of the State Welfare Department. He appointed Dovie to handle DHS adoptions.

274. While Marland did not push for any change to adoption legislation, he believed in the process and supported children's issues.

275. Beth Campbell, "Marland's Kin Brands Squatter Camps Worse than City Slums," *Oklahoma City Times* (January 18, 1935), p. 1.

276. _____, "Melton New Director of State Pension Unit," *The Daily Oklahoman* (August 12, 1936), p. 1.

277. Nance was an early-day editor in Marlow, Oklahoma, in southwestern Oklahoma. Then he moved to Walters, and finally, to Purcell, just north of Pauls Valley. He served in the Oklahoma state legislature representing each of the three districts.

278. _____, "Six Babies Go to New Homes in Day," *The Daily Oklahoman*, January 5, 1936, p. 3A.

279. _____, "Who Will Adopt These Little Brothers? Deserted Mother Seeks Home for Them," *Oklahoma City Times* (Nov. 18, 1936), p. 1.

280. _____, "The World's Warm Hearted, Adoptions Assure Us," *Oklahoma City Times* (December 4, 1936), p. 38.

281. *Ibid.*

282. Paul I. Wellman, "Born to Fight: Governor Red Phillips Battles for States' Rights," *The Sunday Star*, undated clipping, Western History Collection of the University of Oklahoma, Box 16, Number 6.

283. *Survey Graphic* and its sister publication, *Survey Mid-Monthly*, were originally launched by Edward T. Devine as a house organ for the New York Charities Organization in 1897. It was called *Charities*, and later changed to *Charities and the Commons*. When Devine hired Kellogg in 1907 to edit the newsletter, he was charged with educating social workers in new casework methods. He began by surveying social problems in Pittsburg, Pennsylvania. Gathering a wide variety of investigative reports, he brought problems such as unsafe working conditions, unfair labor practices, child labor and the lack of parks and recreational areas to his readers. During *Survey Graphic's* 40-plus years of service, Kellogg tried to anticipate community problems and bring them to print for editorial comment. Kellogg's biographer, Clarke A. Chambers, wrote that, in the 1930s, the editor failed to "explore the constitutional and social implications in the assumption of a general police power by the federal government (New Deal legislation)." Clarke A. Chambers,

Paul U. Kellogg and the Survey: Voices for Social Welfare and Social Justice (Minneapolis: University of Minnesota Press, 1971), p. 150.

284. Beulah Amidon, "Sooners in Security," *Survey Graphic*, Vol. 27, Number 4 (April 1938), p. 207.

285. _____, "Problems to Be Considered in Legislation on Adoption as Illustrated by the Law of Selected States," Department of Labor: U. S. Children's Bureau, 1939. Oklahoma State Archives. RG 23-3-2, Box 2 Folder 5.

286. Mary Ruth Colby, "Memorandum on Oklahoma Adoption Law," Department of Labor: U. S. Children's Bureau, October 20, 1938, Oklahoma State Archives 23-3-2, Box 2, Folder 5, p. 4.

287. _____, "Proposed Changes in the Social Security Act: A Report of the Social Security Board to the President and to the Congress of the United States," *Social Security Bulletin* (January 1939), pp. 4-17.

288. _____, "Birth Record Bill is Passed," *The Daily Oklahoman* (February 11, 1939), p. 15.

289. _____, "Public Assistance in the States," in the *Social Work Year Book 1939* (New York: Russell Sage Foundation, 1939), p. 562

290. Telephone interview with the late Governor Turner's grandson.

291. _____, "Would-Be Foster Mother Has Everything Ready," *Oklahoma City Times* (May 20, 1939), p. 7.

End Notes for Chapter 13 (Children's Issues in the Legislature)

292. _____, "Service Man Seeks Babies For Adoption," *Oklahoma City Times* (December 8, 1939), p. 18.

293. _____, "Minco Couple Wants Baby For Adoption," *Oklahoma City Times* (January 18, 1940), p. 10.

294. _____, "Service Man Gets Offer to Adopt Children," *Oklahoma City Times* (January 8, 1940), p. 5.

295. _____, "Law Change Asked On Child Adoption," *Oklahoma City Times* (March 13, 1940), p. 9.

296. Henry Burchfiel, "Buck Cook Proposes Penal Policy Changes," *Oklahoma City Times* (July 26, 1946), p. 4.

297. _____, "Coe Would Establish Child Welfare Court," *The Daily Oklahoman* (June 13, 1946), p. 7.

298. Letter from William S. Tyson, Acting Solicitor of Labor to Randall S. Cobb, Oklahoma Attorney General, Oklahoma State Capitol Library's Vertical Files.

299. _____, "Board in Past, She Still Puts Family First," *Oklahoma City Times* (January 1, 1947), p. 10.

300. _____, "Baby Bartering Target of Bill in Legislature," *Oklahoma City Times* (February 21, 1947), p. 14.

301. _____, "House Temper Flares in Baby Racket Debate," *The Daily Oklahoman* (March 5, 1947), p. 1.

302. James A. Garvey, "Head of Charities Hits Adoption Bill...It Would Handicap His Work," *Southwest Courier* (January 11, 1947), p. 1.

303. King Features Syndicate, "Stamping Out the Sale of Babies," *Oklahoma City Times* (February 4, 1947), p. 16.

304. *Ibid.*

305. *Ibid.*

306. Edith Johnson, "Gentlemen of the Senate!" *The Daily Oklahoman* (April 1, 1947), p. 8.

307. *Ibid.*

308. _____, "Adoption Bill To Be Revised," *The Daily Oklahoman* (March 28, 1947), p. 3.

309. _____, "Child Adoption Substitute Bill Gains Support," *The Daily Oklahoman* (April 2, 1947), p. 20.

310. _____, "Senate Votes Own Version of Baby Code," *The Daily Oklahoman* (April 3, 1947), p. 1.

311. _____, "Sapulpa Baby Case is Taken to State Court," *Sapulpa Herald* (January 23, 1947), p. 1.

312. Laura Dester, *The Halo Girls: The Story of Oklahoma's Child Welfare Division, 1936-1968* (Oklahoma City, Oklahoma: Oklahoma DHS Publication Number 82-67), p. 37.

313. *Ibid.*, p. 52.

314. Laura Dester, *Annual Report of Child Welfare*, Oklahoma State Archives, RF 23-3-1, Box 2-15, p. 23.

315. _____, "Child Welfare Bill Will Be Introduced," *Wewoka Times-Democrat* (March 20, 1949), p. 1.

316. Investigator X, "Under the Guise of Welfare—Oklahoma Breeding a Society of Illegitimates and Chiselers," *The Tulsa Tribune* (February 6, 1951), p. 1.

317. _____, "Mother Finds Son Left on Tulsa Street in 1929," *The Tulsa Tribune* (August 31, 1951), p. 1.

318. _____, "Foster Father Brands Story of Search for Son False," *The Tulsa Tribune* (September 1, 1951), p. 1.

319. Johnston Murray, "Your State Affairs," *Wewoka Times-Democrat* (February 7, 1952), p. 8.

End Notes for Chapter 14 (A Thriving Maternity Home)

320. _____, "Agencies Tell City Woman She Is Too Old to Adopt a Child," *Oklahoma City Times* (May 20, 1939), p. 7.

321. _____, "Forty-Year-Old 'Mother'–Empty Cradle Filled at Last," *Oklahoma City Times* (July 22, 1939), p. 1. The caption under the picture reminded readers that Mae had purchased a complete layette for a baby after local adoption agencies refused to allow her to adopt because of her age. "Mrs. Harry Marshall...obtained (the baby) direct from the parents."

322. The movie is available for viewing on-site at the Library of Congress, Washington, D.C. Dr. Jordan, played by Ralph Morgan, enlists the aid of an attorney to help him avoid criminal prosecution for selling an illegitimate baby. A gangster hears about the deal, deciding it would make a good racket. He sets up a maternity home, with the doctor and a lawyer as his partners. When the gangster is killed during an argument, Dr. Jordan is blamed. Although he is ultimately freed of the murder charge, he must stand trial for selling babies.

323. _____, "Personals," *The Daily Oklahoman* (October 3, 1948), p. B9.

324. _____, "Mae Marshall, Carson Subpoenaed By Kefauver Subcommittee," *Edmond Booster* (June 2, 1955), p. 1.
325. Mae Marshall's records have never been found. She admitted receiving $100 per birthmother per month. Her "take" has never been verified. It is thought to be significantly higher.

End Notes for Chapter 15 (Sheriff's Knock)

326. _____, "Baby Adoption Ring Hearing Full of Quips," *The Daily Oklahoman* (July 16, 1955), p. 1.
327. _____, "Kefauver's Committee Hears City Pair Testify," *Oklahoma City Times* (July 16, 1955), p. 1.
328. _____, "Quickie Deals For Adoptions Told at Quiz," *The Daily Oklahoman* (July 17, 1955), p. 1.
329. _____, "Kefauver Thanks Marshall, Carson," *Edmond Booster* (July 28, 1955), p. 1. No known relationship exists between Mae and J. B. Marshall, Edmond's city manager.
330. Invoices for these six cases were found in the Vertical File of the El Reno Oklahoma Public Library in El Reno, Oklahoma.
331. Perhaps it is a coincidence, but Daniel B. Purvis reports the same Dr. William B. Catto performed an appendectomy in 1930 on the wife of Lloyd E. Rader, Sr., the director of Oklahoma's Department of Public Welfare (1951–1982). At the time, Mrs. Rader was three months pregnant. Daniel B. Purvis, *Lloyd E. Rader, Sr. – The Early Years that Developed the Character of an Oklahoma Welfare Pioneer*, a thesis in partial fulfillment of Master of Arts in American History/ Museum Studies, Central State Graduate Studies (April 7, 1988), p. 31.
332. _____, "Hospital Board Moves to Halt 'Market' for Babies," *El Reno Daily Tribune* (February 26, 1956), p. 1.
333. Conley, Claire, "Grey Market Upset...State Hospital To Snarl Baby Adoption Deals," *Oklahoma City Times* (February 25, 1956), p. 1.
334. *Ibid.*
335. _____, "Hospital Group Asks Change in Adoption Laws," *El Reno Daily Tribune* (February 28, 1956), p. 1.

336. Conley, Claire, "Hospital's Adoption Policy Hit," *Oklahoma City Times* (March 6, 1956), p. 1.
337. _____, "Hospital Policy on Babies Applauded," *El Reno Daily Tribune* (March 6, 1956), p. 1.
338. *Ibid.*
339. Oklahoma State Statutes, Title 21, Chapter 32A, p. 531.
340. State of Oklahoma v. Mae Marshall, Common Pleas Court of Oklahoma County, Case #23,481, filed November 8, 1957.
341. Henry Burchfiel, "Charge Filed In Adoption Racket Probe," *Oklahoma City Times* (November 8, 1957), p. 1.
342. Mae Marshall v. Deaconess Hospital, District Court of Oklahoma County, State of Oklahoma, Case No. 143874, filed April 21, 1958.
343. _____, "Closing Unwed Mothers Home," *The Daily Oklahoman* (November 19, 1958), p. 3.
344. The name of Central State University has changed to the University of Central Oklahoma.

INDEX

ABOUT THE AUTHOR

Mary S. Payne is an adoptee and an adoption rights advocate for people who were adopted as children. She has been a private investigator for over 15 years and has served as an Oklahoma Department of Human Services confidential intermediary since its inception in 1997. She has also testified about the impact of adoption before various state legislative committees.

"There's a taboo of silence surrounding adoption. Even now, as an adult, I find it difficult to talk about. *Adoption's Hidden History* is my coming out. I was adopted in the 1940s, after 18 months in foster care. My parents were told I would be 'just like their own child.' While trying to fit in, I continued to feel broken even into adulthood. Getting a copy of my pre-adoption birth record brought a sense of wholeness. After researching my own story, I was consumed with learning every event that precipitated changes in adoption law impacting everyone. Adoption's history is the back story of all six million adopted persons."

Made in the USA
Lexington, KY
19 September 2017